Leadership Is A Way Of Life

Teen Edition

Julie and Charles Fonbuena

Divinative Leadership

Copyright © 2012 by Julie and Charles Fonbuena

Divinative Leadership
www.divinativeleadership.com

ISBN: 978-0-9833610-0-8

All rights reserved. No part of this publication may be reproduced, stored in a retrieval system or transmitted, in any form, or by any means, electronic, mechanical, recorded, photocopied, or otherwise, without the prior written permission of both the copyright owner and the above publisher of this book, except by a reviewer who may quote brief passages in a review.

The scanning, uploading, and distribution of this book via the Internet or via any other means without the permission of the publisher is illegal and punishable by law. Please purchase only authorized electronic editions and do not participate on or encourage electronic piracy of copyrightable materials. Your support of the author's rights is appreciated.

Printed in the United States of America

Acknowledgements

We would like to give a big thanks to our children for being amazing teenagers. At the time of this printing, we have four teenagers in our home.

Way back when our children were young, as we would ask for advice on parenting, we often heard about the terrors of the terrible teens. Yet somewhere along the way we also heard that with the right attitude, living with teens could be an awesome, fun, and fulfilling time of life for the whole family. We choose to listen to the latter advice, and we often told ourselves, our children, and others that we were sure they *would* be awesome years. We truly believed it could be that way, and that is exactly what has happened! They have been amazing! We have loved having teenagers in our home. We love laughing, playing, talking, working, and crying together. We have not been problem free, but we are grateful for everyday that we get to spend with them.

Thanks Leslie, Nathan, Lauren, Leilani, Lindcee, Spencer, and Benjamin for letting us practice our parenting skills on you. And thanks for all your real time feedback and help as we have written this book. You are the best!! We love you!! And we look forward to the few years we have left with teenagers in our home.

Contents

CHAPTER ONE

LEADERSHIP IS A WAY OF LIFE

IF you could choose one word to describe what's it's like to be a teenager, what word would you choose?

As you think about what word you might use, consider that being a teenager *can* be the absolute best time of your life. Think about it. You're not a little kid anymore. You're smarter than you've ever been. Before you were a teenager, your parents could figure out how to help you with your homework no matter what the subject was. By the time you are a teenager your school subjects are more complex and your parents know less and less about the stuff you are studying.

Not only are you smarter, but you are also taller, stronger, and faster than you've ever been before. As a teenager you are mature enough that you don't have to have your parents or someone else escort you everywhere. You have more independence now. Your curfew is later than it used to be, which means you have more options. You are creating new interests and friendships. You can talk with adults more easily now. You feel more confident you can handle being an adult someday. Some adults even compliment you and let you know you have great potential. Sometimes adults even ask for your opinion, help, and advice.

Of course the big word in the second sentence of this book is *can*. Being a teenager *can* be the best time of your life. It can also be a very tough part of your life. Maybe you are smarter than ever before but school is getting tougher every semester. Maybe you are taller, stronger, and faster than ever before, but maybe too often you don't feel very good physically. Maybe you are more independent and can go to more places, but you're not quite sure where to go. Maybe you have gone all over the place and discovered there are fewer and fewer exciting places to go. Maybe your circle of friends and interests are expanding but somehow you don't feel like you quite fit in. Maybe instead of others asking you questions to get your opinion, you may feel like you are just being interrogated. Maybe instead of people asking for you advice, they prefer just telling you what to do. Maybe getting closer to being a grown-up was exciting at first but the more you find out, it seems like being an adult is just more work with less flexibility and more responsibility with less fun.

So what is the difference between your teenage years being the best time of your life, or your teenager years *not* being the best time of your life? In a word: *leadership*.

You might ask, "Really? Is that it? Is that all? What does that mean exactly?"

Leadership is one of those words that people define differently—like *beauty*, *happiness*, or *success*. Even if people do come to an agreement as to what the word *leadership* means, what are you supposed to do with it?

In this book we will define what leadership is, and we will explore how *your* leadership has affected your life in the past, how it is affecting you now, and how it will affect you into the future from this point forward.

Here is the way we will define leadership:

Leadership is lifting others to the standards you are inspired to earnestly live.

A lot of meaning goes into that sentence. There are four parts to our definition of leadership.

- The first part says that to be a leader, you need to have standards.
- Second, leadership means the standards you have identified are important and inspirational enough that you earnestly strive to consistently live your life according to those standards. By the way, *earnestly* means you are willing to put in work and effort to make leadership real in your life. Leadership first asks you to lead your own life and make leadership part of who you are.
- Third, only as you strive to understand and live the first two aspects of leadership can you have empathy for what others need in order to be uplifted.
- Fourth, not only are you lifting others, but more specifically, you are

lifting them toward the same standards by which you are inspired to live. This fourth part asks you to not only live for yourself but also to lift and improve other people's lives.

Before going into more detail, let's take a look at the questions this book will attempt to help you answer.

- Can everyone be a leader? If everyone can be a leader, who's the follower?
- What is leadership and what exactly are leaders supposed to be and do?
- How can I become a better leader?
- What is the difference between being a leader and just being popular?
- I watch the news and sometimes someone who is supposed to be a leader ends up being a crook and a fraud. What's up with that? How will I know a legit leader versus a fake?
- How will leadership help me now and in the future?
- Where do I start?

This is just a short list and you probably have other questions. Jot them down and we'll see how many of them we can help you answer.

There will be a quiz at the end of each chapter. This will help you remember the main points of the chapter. Here are a few questions on your first quiz for this opening chapter.

Your teenage years

a) Are guaranteed to be the absolute best time of your life.
b) Are guaranteed to be the absolute worst time of your life.
c) *Can* be the best time of your life.

What will make the difference between your teenage years being the best time of your life versus not the best time of your life?

a) Popularity
b) Better teachers
c) Leadership
d) Luck

Leadership is lifting others to the standards you are inspired to earnestly live.

a) True
b) False

I'm sure you did well on the quiz. In that little quiz you answered some pretty big and powerful questions. Well done! If you want to get the most out of this book, another thing you can do after you take the quiz is to share what you have learned with another person. It will help you remember what you have learned and you'll probably have some interesting discussions too. Let's move on.

CHAPTER TWO

AN OVERVIEW OF OUR DEFINITION OF LEADERSHIP

THE simple picture below will remind you what leadership is, what the different parts of leadership are, and how each part relates to one another. It is made of three intersecting circles and three lines forming a triangle. Each of the three lines of the triangle starts from the middle of the three circles. As you read this book, you can use this picture to quickly determine how you are currently doing with your leadership abilities, celebrate what you are doing well, and decide what adjustments you may need to make.

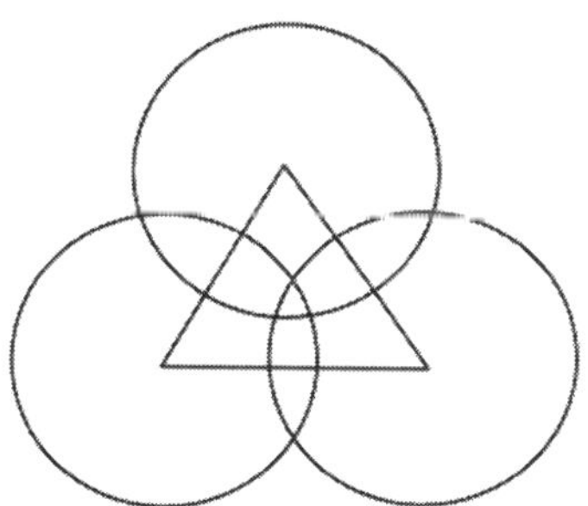

There are four parts to this leadership model. The first part of this leadership model is called the "The Mind of a Leader." In our three circles and triangle picture, the three circles together represent the mind of the leader. The top circle represents the standards that you want to live by as a leader. The left circle represents you, and the right circle represents other people, whether family, friends, or any other person.

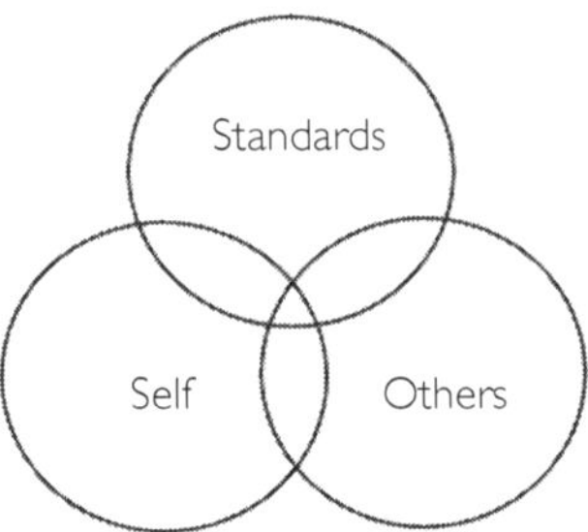

The Mind of a Leader is one that considers all three of these components together. Each is important and even more important is for a leader to understand how each of these three components relates to each other.

The second part is called "The Integrity of a Leader." In our picture The Integrity of a Leader is the left line of the triangle. This line connects the circle representing you and the circle representing the standards you want to live by. The Integrity of a Leader draws the leader closer to the standard he or she wants to live by and keeps him or her there.

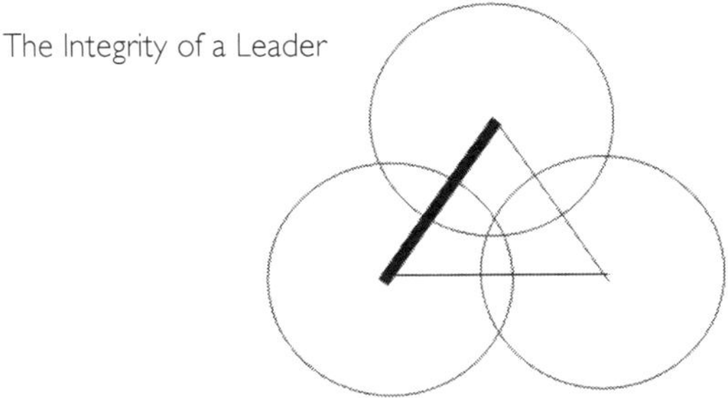

More than making sure the leader lives close to his/her self-chosen standards, The Integrity of a Leader represented by this line, should be such that the circle representing you and the circle representing the standards you want to live by overlap, meaning the standards you want to live by are not something separate from you but the standards you want to live by is part of who you are. The purpose behind The Integrity of a Leader is to make sure the standard you want to live by is woven and integrated into your life.

The third part is called "The Heart of a Leader." In our leadership model, The Heart of a Leader is the bottom line of the triangle. This line connects the circle representing you and the circle representing others. Having a heart of a leader is about how well you connect with others as people, regardless of what leadership positions you may or may not have. The circle representing you and the circle representing others are not just close, but they overlap as well. This means you care enough about others and they are important enough to you, that you feel they are a part of you and not just another face in the crowd. When we cover The Heart of a Leader in greater depth and detail, we will outline specific things you can be and do to strengthen the bond you have with others.

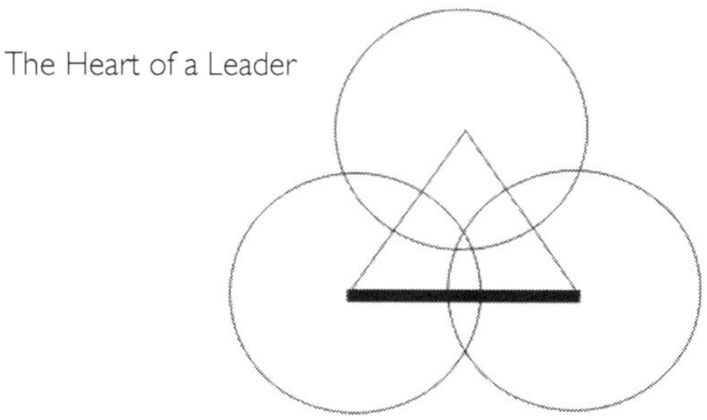

The fourth part is called "The Legacy of a Leader." In our leadership picture, The Legacy of a Leader is represented by the right side of the triangle. This line connects the circle representing others with the circle representing the standards you want to live by. The Legacy of a Leader is to connect others to the same standards the leader is inspired to earnestly live. The intent of this line is to remind you that there are very specific things you can do as a leader to help family, friends and loved ones to be the very best they can be. You can see that the circle representing others and the circle representing the standards you want to live by also overlap. This will help you as a leader know how well you are leading others by how well other people live according to inspired standards.

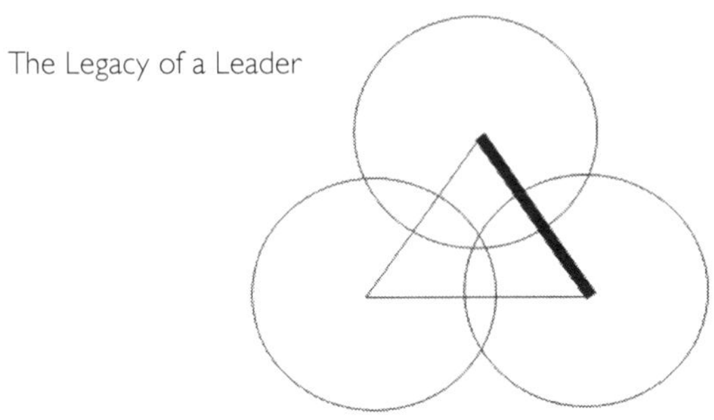

Let's go back briefly to our definition of leadership.

Leadership is lifting others to the standards you are inspired to earnestly live.

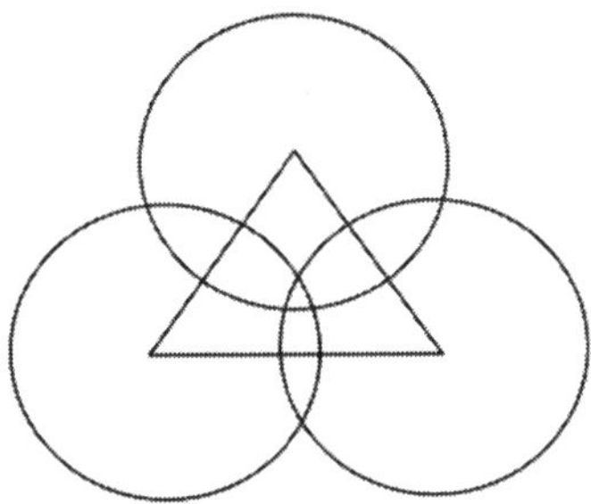

Our leadership picture and the definition of the word *leadership* above fit together. As we explore this definition with our simple leadership picture, you will know exactly what leadership is and how to develop your leadership abilities. As the title of this book indicates: *Leadership is a Way of Life*. This book will give you a roadmap to make leadership a way of living your life, and in the process, help you awaken your awesomeness within.

You've just gotten a really quick overview or our definition of leadership. We'll come back and give you more details on each of these parts of leadership. Before doing that, however, there are two sets of concepts we need to cover first.

If you look at the subtitle of this book it reads *Awaken Your Awesomeness Within*. Awaken is an interesting word. I love to take naps whenever I get a chance because when I take a nap, I am relaxed and worry-free, and I wake up refreshed. However, when I take too long of a nap, I actually wake up tired, weak, and low on energy, which seems kind of weird, because I haven't been doing anything. I chose the word *awaken* because too often we live our lives as if we're in a long mental nap—we may be a bit tired, weak, low of energy, and feel an overall "blah." When I nap too long I certainly don't feel my awesomeness when I wake up.

In the first set of concepts I'll cover five ideas that are so cool and interesting that they will awaken your awesomeness within. By the way, your awesomeness is not something that is outside of you. It is already in you even though you may not even know it. Your awesomeness may be "taking a nap." We'll wake up the awesome that is within you.

The second set of concepts we need to cover before we revisit our leadership model involves six strategies that will be explained through six allegories. An allegory is a story or a symbol. Allegories are intended to make something that may be difficult to understand, easier to learn and remember. Allegories can also be compared to fables or parables.

After we go through these two sets of concepts, we'll revisit our leadership model and give you greater insights on leadership. You will then examine some scenarios where you will apply what you have learned. You will be pleasantly surprised at just how much awesomeness you already possess.

Have you ever studied something in school, learned it pretty well, and then realized by the time you took the test, just how much you had forgotten. Or even worse, from the time school is out for the summer, to when it starts again the following school year, you forget even more. Well, the reason you may forget is because you may not be applying what you have learned consistently enough to remember it, especially over the summer. By giving you an opportunity to apply your leadership skills, knowledge, and talents on a weekly basis, not only will you remember these leadership principles, but your life will be better for it. Leadership is one subject you will always need for the rest of your life. In the last part of this book there is a tool that you can use so that you won't forget what we have covered. Not only will you remember what we have covered, but you'll also learn how to implement it and make leadership a part of your life every week in a very simple and powerful way. This tool is intended to help you make leadership an integral part of your life. You'll be amazed at what a difference it will make.

Chapter Quiz:

The three circles in the leadership picture represent

a) Three connected cinnamon rolls
b) The mind of the leader
c) Just random shapes
d) All of the above

The three lines that make up the triangle represent The Integrity of a Leader, The Heart of a Leader, and The Legacy of a Leader.

a) True
b) False

CHAPTER THREE

THREE BRAINS

THE first set of concepts is five cool and exciting ideas designed to awaken your awesomeness within. They are

- Three Brains
- The Ugly Duckling
- The Distance Between Heaven and Hell
- Pre-forgiveness
- The Weave of Life: To-be and To-do

Let's start with the three brains. The neurologist (a doctor who focuses on the brain, spine, nerves, and muscles) Paul MacLean has proposed in his book *The Triune Brain in Evolution,* that our skulls hold not one but three brains. You can look at them as three connected computers, where each computer has its own intelligence and memory.

Lizard-Brain

MacLean refers to one part of the brain as the reptilian brain. It's also called the lower brain, but in this book we'll refer to it as the *lizard-brain.* This is the brain stem and cerebellum that controls the movement of your muscles as well as balance, breathing, and heartbeat. He refers to it as the reptilian brain, because with reptiles, this is the dominant part of their brain; it controls their survival instincts, behavior, and thinking. It basically responds to two questions: *Can I eat it?* or *Can it eat me?* After those two questions are answered, the brain then operates on survival instincts and asks: *How do I conquer my prey or escape from being conquered?*

Monkey-Brain

The second brain he refers to is the limbic system. It's also called the middle brain. The limbic system includes parts of our brain with fancy names such as the amygdala, the hypothalamus, and the hippocampus. The limbic system has also been referred to as the mammalian brain, but in this book we'll refer to it as the *monkey*-brain. This part of the human brain is home to our feelings, emotions and moods. As these scientists studied the brain they found that at the touch of an electrode to this part of our brain, we can feel fear, pleasure, joy, and rage. In this limbic system or emotional system everything is either "agreeable or disagreeable." This is the part of the brain that tells us to avoid pain from whatever the source we don't like, regardless of whether it's good or bad. For example, if you don't like broccoli, this is the part of the brain that says to avoid broccoli, because you don't feel good when you are eating broccoli even if broccoli may be good for your physical health. The monkey-brain also tells you to repeat pleasure from whatever the source regardless of whether or not it is good for you. For example, have you ever gotten in trouble for doing something you thought was funny like pulling a prank on your brother, sister, or friend? You probably didn't do it with the intent to get into trouble. You did it because you thought it was funny at the time.

The limbic system of our brain is not only connected to the decisions we make with our emotions, but it is also connected to how we interact with others. Just as there are rules regarding how monkeys, dolphins, and other mammals interact with each other, this is the part of your brain that tells you there are certain rules and certain things you do or not do when you're interacting with other people. This part of the brain reinforces the idea that if you want to fit in with others, you need to follow the rule of the pack. When we feel that we belong in the pack, we feel better; when we feel that we are on the outside looking in and not part of the pack, we don't feel so good.

Divine-Brain

MacLean refers to the third part of the human brain as the neocortex. The neocortex makes up about two-thirds of the total brain mass of a human. In animals, however, the neocortex is much smaller than the other two brains. MacLean refers to the neocortex as "the mother of invention and father of abstract thought." The neocortex is where higher-level thinking occurs. This includes language, music, math, planning, memory storage, the processing of complex information, communication, and so forth. You would add to that list other higher-level thinking such as principles, inspiration, love, purpose, contribution, and other abstract ideas that don't exist with other species. This part of the human brain is what separates us from the rest of the animal kingdom. All of the technological advances, inventions, and the creation of other conveniences that you enjoy today were processed through the neocortex. All three brains serve an important purpose. We wouldn't want be without any of them.

Sun, Moon and Stars

If you think about all the cool things that you and I have around us that we may take for granted, such as the latest fancy phones, computer games, television, microwave oven, power everything in cars, and computers, it is really quite remarkable. How you ever watched television shows where they explain how buildings, rockets, planes, clothes and even how our food is made? It's surprising how much knowledge, innovation, and technology goes in to them.

If as a species, humans have progressed that far, why is it that animals haven't invented similar things? It's because the brains of animals are not as sophisticated as humans. The human brain is more capable than the animal brain. When you consider how sophisticated the human brain is compared to the mammalian (monkey) or reptilian (lizard) brain, you could draw comparisons to the brightness of the stars, the moon, and the sun. The brightness of the stars is like the lizard-brain. There is obviously intelligence there but certainly less intelligence than in the more sophisticated mammal. Just as the moon is significantly brighter than the stars as you look in the night sky, so is the mammalian brain so much more intelligent than the lizard-brain. It is interesting to note that even though the brightness of the moon is greater than the stars, we mostly see both of them at night. The brightness of the sun, however, we see during the day. Because the sun is so bright, it's difficult if not impossible to see the moon or stars during the day, and yet, they are still out there. The sun is thousands of times brighter than the moon and the stars.

Likewise, the neocortex is not just *significantly* more intelligent than our other brains—but *infinitely* more so. Let the brightness of the sun serve as a reminder to you each day to use your most intelligent brain, your neocortex. With it you will see yourself, others, and your opportunities more clearly. Much of society, however—from schools, neighborhoods, video games, the shows you watch on television and in movies, and even sports teams—is primarily set up as lizard-brain places where "eat or be eaten" or "compete and conquer" thinking dominate. You need to make a conscious and deliberate effort to use your most intelligent brain. It can be done, and to help you realize your best self, your awesome self—it must be done. To remind us of the immense potential and brightness of the human brain, I'll refer to the neocortex portion of the human brain as the divine-brain.

One Brain Will Dominate

MacLean discovered something interesting about the relationships among the three brains. The way your three brains relate to each other creates your view of the world. Your view of the world will affect how you lead your life, how you will lead others, and what you will choose to do with your time. The more you understand how your three-part brain works, the more you will realize why you make certain decisions and you'll discover what is truly important in your life. Let's go back to the three brains and take a look at how they are interrelated.

Here's the big "aha." One of these three brains can dominate the other two! This means our reptile brain can dominate our thinking, and we view the world at the survival level: *Can I eat it*? or *Can it eat me*? This can be the case even with someone who has a highly-developed limbic system and neocortex. In other words, have you ever met people who are really smart (get good grades and seem to have all the answers), have the ability to get along well with people (they're probably popular), but seem to use all their intelligence to prove they are better than somebody else or they are always trying to beat someone else at something—anything—even if no one cares or asks?

With a person who is lizard-brain dominant, everything is about competition or trying to prove how one person might be better than the next person, and there is always comparison. When a person's lizard-brain is the dominant brain, it's not enough to look *good*; it's about looking *better* than the next person. With lizard-brain thinking it's not enough to be *smart*; it's about being the *smartest* of the smart. It's not about being *liked*; it's about being the *most popular* and making sure someone else isn't as popular. It's about always being the winner in whatever these people do. Survival and conquest become more important than anything else in their lives.

This mindset may even dominate every aspect of their lives. They're in the survival, conquest, and competitive mode at school with other students, at home with parents and siblings, whether they are playing a sport, just playing with friends, playing computer games, and even while driving on the road. They see the world as primarily a competitive "eat or be eaten" environment. As you think about what it means to be lizard-brain focused, don't limit yourself to people you know personally. As you study current events or hear stories in the news, do you see examples of people who are lizard-brain focused? As you study and learn about different people in your history classes, can you come up with examples of people who are lizard-brain focused?

Please don't get me wrong when I say this. I recognize that it can be tough out there and you need to survive. In fact, you want to develop your lizard-brain; just make sure it's not your dominant brain. Survival may be part of the current reality in too much of the world around you and me, but life is more than just surviving. There are parts of the world that are very tough and violent and it may seem as though everyone is only in it for themselves, but even in these places we hear stories of hope and inspiration. So it's not the environment we are in or the actions and attitudes of other people that decide what we ultimately do. What is critically important is to be aware of which part of our three-part brain is dominating our thinking.

Going back to our leadership picture of three interconnected circles and three lines forming a triangle, lizard-brain thinking is like having most of the picture missing; there is only one circle. It's not about standards. It's not about others. It's not about making connections. It's about thinking about "me" first and foremost with a focus on simply surviving or trying to be better than everyone else.

Even if the reptilian brain or lizard-brain is not in charge, the other concern is when the limbic system or monkey-brain dominates the other two brains. This may mean that the pursuit of pleasure may be our dominant thinking and goal. It's all about having fun or doing whatever feels good at the given moment. Using our monkey-brains as our dominant brain could also mean we tend to make decisions based on avoiding pain or discomfort even if the present discomfort would end up being better for us in the long run. It could also mean going along with what everybody else is doing to fit in, even when the divine-brain says it's not a good idea. Have you ever seen smart people do dumb things? Sometimes we make decisions based on what feels good at the moment without using our higher or divine level of thinking. Have you ever asked a friend at school after she made a big, obvious mistake, and you knew she was more than capable of figuring it out, "What were you *thinking*?" Have you ever wondered why you may also do dumb things—and not only that, but you do the same dumb things over and over again? You may even say to yourself, "I know better than to do that!" It may be helpful to change the question from, "What was I thinking?" to

"Which one of my three brains dominated my thinking?"

Too often the lizard-brain or the monkey-brain is the mastermind behind our actions, but the divine-brain gets the blame.

Consider this scenario. Walking home from school with kids in the neighborhood, in the course of the conversations, Robert makes fun of how Stephanie looks. It isn't a very nice thing to say but other kids laugh, and so Robert feels like he is funny and feels accepted (monkey-brain) because others laughed; thus he assumes it's okay and keeps saying mean things hoping to get more laughs from others. Of course Stephanie feels bad, says nothing, and thinks Robert is a jerk; she will probably hate him for life (lizard-brain). Later on, Robert is thinking about what he did and knows he was mean. The next day he apologizes to Stephanie (divine-brain). You probably see these types of interactions happen hundreds of times every day. Be aware and be careful. Our monkey-brains are so powerful that they can actually hold our divine-brains (the most intelligent brain) hostage.

Have you ever wondered how it is possible that on the one hand some people live inspirational lives, while on the other hand some people live their lives with more cruelty and violence than anything that is seen in the animal kingdom? It can be traced back to the strength of each of the three parts of our brains. Whether we live an inspirational life or a life wishing we were better, depends on which of our three brains dominates our thinking.

Going back to our leadership picture of three interconnected circles and three lines forming a triangle, monkey-brain thinking is like having only the two circles representing you and others. That kind of thinking leaves out the standards you want to live by, and it also leaves out the lines that make the connections strong with each circle. Again, the monkey-brain focus is about doing what feels good in the moment without any other consideration. Why would someone eat junk food until he feel gross, play video games for hours, watch television endlessly, surf the web without purpose, or text constantly without having anything meaningful to say? Although there may be unwanted consequences later, many have done these activities simply because it feels good at the moment.

Another common monkey-brain activity is to do whatever it takes just to fit in with others. This includes the way people talk, walk, what they say, what clothes they wear, what their hair style is, who they hang out with, or who they don't want to be seen with. Remember, feeling good and fitting in are not necessarily bad things. The question is whether we are monkey-brain dominant.

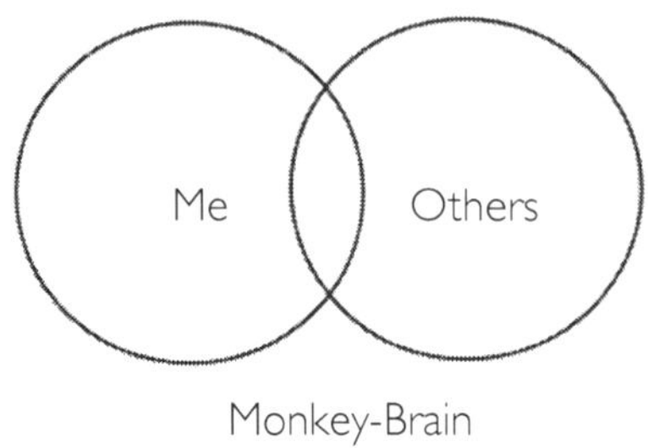

It's about doing what makes me feel good.
It's about fitting in and not being on the outside looking in.

Be Divinative

The best alternative is to make sure that our divine-brain dominates our thinking. The more I thought about this the more I wanted to try and find the right word, the right adjective, to describe being absolutely sure, intentional, careful, and deliberate in our determination to have our divine-brains be our dominant brains. I wanted to find the word that captures the very best that exists in each of us. I wanted to find a word to describe the deliberate use of our divine-brains. Because I couldn't find the right word, I came up with a new word. The word is "divinative." Be *divinative* in your thoughts and feelings. Be *divinative* in your words and actions. Be *divinative* in how you lead your life and in how you choose to spend your time.

Being divinative means using your divine-brain as your dominant brain.

Remember that all three of our brains are interconnected, and each serves an important purpose. We wouldn't want to be without any of the three. The key is to have our divine-brains dominate our thinking rather than to allow our lizard-brains or monkey-brains to dominate. That does not mean we should try to go around and bypass our lizard-brains and monkey-brains, because they are interconnected and are also necessary. It's also important to remember that our lizard-brains and monkey-brains need to be developed. Our lizard-brains—meaning our skills, talents, and instincts to survive in this competitive world—need to be developed. Our monkey-brain intelligence of getting along well with people is a worthwhile skill, and it is also a talent to develop.

Interestingly, even lizards and monkeys have all three brains just like humans, but the neocortex of a human is so much larger in relation to the reptilian and mammalian brains than any other creature on earth. The key is to develop habits where the neocortex or divine-brains, dominate our thinking. Our goal then is to lead our lives and use our time with the intent to develop our most intelligent divine-brains. When you do this you will realize the type of leader you want to be, and awaken your awesomeness within.

Thinking of our leadership picture with the three interconnected circles and the three lines forming a triangle, divine-brain thinking includes all three circles. It is interesting to look at the symbolism of circles. This leadership model could have been three squares, three rectangles, three oblongs, or three of any other shape. The symbolism of the circle, however, is perfection and infinity. I believe with all my heart and mind that everyone is perfect. When I say perfect, I'm not referring to someone who has no faults or weaknesses. Too many of us get caught up in this definition and goal of being free of fault. Look at the word *perfect* another way. When looking at the 13th century definition of the adjective *perfect*, it means complete. The 14th century definition of the verb *perfect* means to bring to full development.

Every person is complete or they have everything they need to be their very best. Every person has infinite potential. You have greatness within you. There are contributions to be made in this world that only you can make. Every person has unique talents and skills that the rest of the world needs to see.

Look at it another way. Imagine your dream car for a moment. Really! Take a moment to imagine what it would be like if you could have your dream car right now. Imagine the color and the shine on your brand new dream car. Imagine what it would be like to sit on the driver's seat—probably leather. Imagine the colors inside the car. Imagine your hands on the steering wheel. Picture the speedometer and all the other gauges. Picture the sound system in the car. Think about what music you might be listening to in your brand new dream car. Imagine the smell of your new dream car. Imagine where you would like to drive it. Now imagine *never* turning the ignition key on and never starting the car. That's kind of a downer thought, isn't it?

Although everyone is perfect, too many people never turn on the ignition, if you will, to their perfect or complete life. One the purposes of this book, is to help you figure out how to fully realize the potential of your unique and perfect life—to awaken your awesomeness within. It begins with understanding how our wonderful brains work as represented by these three interconnected circles. You are perfect. Others are perfect. The divine-brain standards you choose to live by are also perfect. That is why we have these three circles.

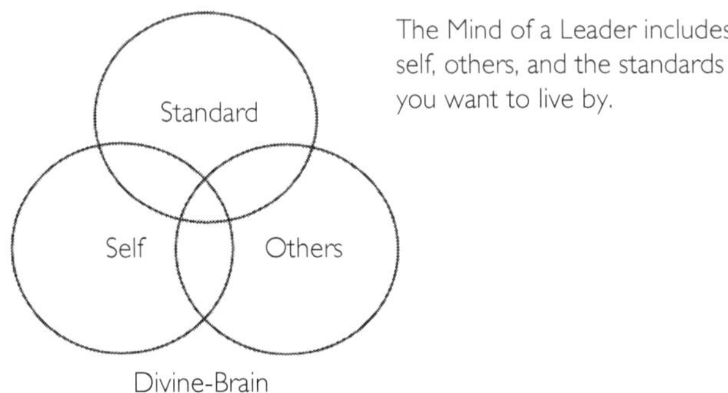

The Mind of a Leader includes self, others, and the standards you want to live by.

Hopefully you can appreciate why understanding your three brains is an important idea in awakening your awesomeness within. We all need to look at ourselves and ask which brain dominates our thinking. Regardless of whichever one dominates your thinking now, what is even more important is deciding which one you want to dominate your thinking from this day forward. We've covered the first of five cool ideas that will awaken your awesomeness within. The second idea is based on the fairy tale *The Ugly Duckling*. We'll cover that in the next chapter.

Chapter Quiz:

The three brains referred to in this chapter are

1 - ________________ Brain or Reptilian Brain
2 - ________________ Brain or Mammalian Brain
3 - ________________ Brain or Neocortex

The big "aha" when it comes to the three brains is that one of them can ____________ the other two!

The lizard-brain responds to two questions. The first is, "Can I eat it?' and the second question is, "_____________________?"

The monkey-brain responds to two additional questions. The first is, "Does it feel good or not feel good?" and the other is, "Do I fit in or not fit in?"

a) True
b) False

Being divinative means your divine-brain or neocortex is your dominant brain.

a) True
b) False

CHAPTER FOUR

THE UGLY DUCKLING

THE *Ugly Duckling* is a famous fairy tale by Danish author Hans Christian Andersen. The tale begins with a mother duck waiting patiently for her eggs to hatch. One by one the eggs hatch until there is only one left, which takes an unusually long time to hatch. When it finally hatches, the creature is large, ugly, and peculiar. Perceived as homely, it endures a great deal of physical and verbal abuse—not just from the ducks, but other farm animals as well. Even the girl who had to feed the poultry kicked it. Saddened, he wanders from the barn and lives with wild ducks and geese; they are not any kinder than those in the barn. After enduring more ridicule, he ends up going into the home of an old woman with her cat and hen who tease him mercilessly. Sad and alone he declares to the cat and hen as he leaves, "You don't understand me." He sees a flock of wild swans and marvels at their beauty and strength. He had not seen such birds before. He is excited to see the swans, but he cannot join them. Winter arrives, and he spends a miserable winter alone. When spring finally arrives, he sees his reflection on the water, and he is no longer the gray and ugly duckling but has matured into a beautiful swan. He is welcomed into a flock of beautiful swans.

I love the ending of this story:

> He had been persecuted and despised for his ugliness, and now he heard them say he was the most beautiful of all the birds. Even the elder-tree bent down its bows into the water before him, and the sun shone warm and bright. Then he rustled his feathers, curved his slender neck, and cried joyfully, from the depths of his heart, "I never dreamed of such happiness as this, while I was an ugly duckling."

When you look at this fairy tale and the reality of the three parts of our brains, you can come away with two lessons. The first lesson is about understanding how much influence others have on you and me. Remember the monkey-brain. We have a strong desire to fit in and to belong. The ugly duckling was influenced by other animals, no matter where he went and no matter the setting. The ugly duckling was affected by others in four different settings. The first setting was with those who knew him from birth. The second setting was with extended family and friends. The third was with new friends. The fourth was with a completely new setting and environment when it came to the old woman, cat and hen. One setting was no better than the next. He was equally sad, disregarded, and mistreated no matter where he went. At the end of all this, he correctly concludes, "You don't understand me."

Similarly, simply being in a new environment or around new people may not change how others see you and me, nor determine whether we are accepted or not. In other words, even though the highly intelligent divine-brain (neocortex) is capable of so much, this ability is made to seem less important when we don't have the approval of others (monkey-brain). Remember the ugly duckling's words, "You don't understand me." The ugly duckling was saying in essence, "you don't *understand* the very best that is in me or you're not helping me *realize* the very best that is in me." This works both ways, however. If we can surround ourselves with people who can support and encourage the most intelligent and divine within us, we can do and be so much more than we even realize.

The second lesson is the realization that our greatest power is the power to choose. Consider the end of the tale when the ugly duckling declared,

> I never dreamed of such happiness as this, while I was an ugly duckling.

Once the ugly duckling realized he was a swan, everything changed. How he viewed himself changed, and how others viewed him vastly improved as well. Granted, this is a fairy tale, and the transformation or change was a physical transformation. You may be asking yourself, "Can *every* part of my life be transformed?" Absolutely! The answer lies first in realizing that you may have been held back by the feedback and clues from your lizard-brain (everything is about survival) and your monkey-brain (everything is about whether you're feeling good or bad, whether you're accepted by others or what your other emotions demand). Relying on acceptance from other people means you are limited by what others say you are and you can only be as good as others say you are. However, when you use more of your divine-brain (neocortex) you will realize you are much more. The divine human brain (neocortex) makes up two-thirds of the total brain mass. Until we tap into the vast capabilities of the most intelligent part of ourselves—the divine-brain—we are living well below our potential. It would be like walking in the dimmer light of the moon or stars, when walking in the brightness of the noon day sun is an option.

Everything we need, we already have and have always had—and it is so important that it is even protected by our skulls. Leadership begins with being divinative. We just need to tap into the divine part of our brain. Again, be divinative. When we look at people who are role models throughout history, they collectively stand as proof and evidence of what is possible if we can tap into our divine-brain and focus on being the very best people and leaders we can be. The great lesson of the fairy tale *The Ugly Duckling* as it relates to understanding that leadership is a way of life is this:

You have the power to make choices!

You have the power to choose to see yourself differently. You have the power to say no to lizard-brain and monkey-brain dominant thoughts. You have the power to say yes to divinative thoughts. You have the power to let go of ugly duckling messages from others and focus on seeing the great swan in you, metaphorically speaking.

The opposite of not realizing you have the power to choose is to blame everything and everyone else for what is not going well. For example how many of the following phrases have you heard before or perhaps you may have said them yourself?

- He makes me so mad.
- She's being mean to me.
- They started it.
- They won't let me do anything.

While it is true that others can influence what happens to you, even in difficult situations you can still choose how you will respond. At the very least you can come up with some creative options. The words that come out of someone who is divinative may start off with phrases such as:

- What if …
- Let's try it this way.
- I wonder if we could …
- Oh, I know …

NEED A NEW COACH AND TEACHER

Think of being more divinative another way. As a teenager you have probably participated for years now in school, sports, music, work or some combination of all of these activities. Over the years you know that some of your coaches and teachers are better than others. Every now and then, however, you get an exceptional coach or teacher, and everything changes. Think about your favorite teacher or coach. Write his or her name in the space below.

My favorite coach or teacher is: ______________________________.

As you think about your favorite teacher or coach have you noticed that you learn more with that person? You learn faster and learning is more enjoyable. You have more success and it is exciting. Remember, you are still the same person. So if you are still the same person, how can the results be so different? The difference is the teacher or coach. The difference is with the person who is in charge of helping you develop and get better. You favorite teacher's approach to learning and teaching makes more sense to you. Your effective coach's approach to practice and games is more disciplined and deliberate. More time is spent on skill development and strategy without losing the element of fun. Their response to mistakes is more helpful. The way the coach or teacher sees each player or student is more uplifting. The players' and students' responses to the coach or teacher are encouraging, inspirational, and fun.

Comparatively, we all have three brains, and each brain has the ability to be the coach and call the shots on how we live our lives. Changing the way we see the world and how we see ourselves and others, can be achieved by simply changing the coach or teacher—the *mental* coach or teacher. Make sure it's the divine-brain calling the shots and not the lizard-brain or monkey-brain. When the most intelligent brain is in charge, we'll see our progress differently. We'll see our setbacks and mistakes differently. We'll approach life with more hope, love, purpose, and forgiveness.

> The greatest lesson of our three brains and the ugly duckling is that we have the power to choose and to put our divine-brains in charge.

This is the single greatest decision that we can make. Once we make the decision to put our divine-brains in charge we'll realize that we can make every other decision. We will realize that we have the freedom to choose. Time and again when people make this shift they feel liberated and would want to exclaim like the ugly duckling,

> I never dreamed of such happiness as this, while I was an ugly duckling.

Making this mental shift or coaching change is something that is going to take some practice, and we will use our leadership strategy as well as a leadership tool to make sure that we do exactly that. We'll talk about that tool in the last section. The habits formed from the lizard-brain and monkey-brain don't just go away immediately, however, and those old habits sneak back in from time to time. Regardless, with some practice and persistence you can become more consistent in having your divine-brain serve as your dominant brain.

> It is only the view from where you sit that makes you feel defeat.
> Life is full of many aisles, so why don't you change your seat?
>
> —Author Unknown

GETTING A DIFFERENT VIEW

In the type of work that I do where I fly all over the country, the airlines give you air miles or points. When you have enough points or air miles you can travel to different places in the world using your points. When we had enough air miles or points, we decided as a family to use our points to go on a vacation to Hawaii.

While we were in Hawaii we thought it would be a great idea to take surfing lessons. The surf instructor even guaranteed that each of us would be able to stand up and surf or we would get our money back. We couldn't pass up the guarantee of being able to surf in Hawaii and we were so excited to try it.

It was hard at first just to stand up because it was tricky to get your balance and we were trying to remember everything the surf instructor had taught us. We kept trying over and over, and after a while it got easier and easier to stand up. The rest of my family was really good, and they could surf as far into shore as they wanted to. I was having a completely different experience altogether, however. I was having a hard time, because even though I could stand up, I would only stand for a few seconds before falling. I would stand and fall over and over again. I could tell the surf instructor was watching me fall time and time again, and she would just scratch her head in disbelief. Finally she wanted to talk to me and give me some advice.

She gave me some advice I will never forget. She said, "Where your eyes go, your body will follow." This was a pretty amazing advice, really. Most novice surfers are good enough to figure out how to stand up and balance, but when they get worried that they might fall, they do. When they looked down to the right, they would fall to the right. When they looked down to the left, they would fall to the left. Where their eyes went, their body followed. She then gave some additional advice. She said after you stand up, don't just look down; instead look up at the palm trees, the sugar cane fields or the mountains. It wasn't until she mentioned it that I realized that the whole time I had been surfing, I had never bothered to look at the beautiful palm trees, mountains, clouds, or the hotels along the shoreline. Why would I continue to just look down at a small patch of water when I could look up at the Hawaiian Islands? Duh!

So what does this surfing story have to do with being divinative or having your divine-brain become your dominant brain? It's about the lens through which you see life. If your dominant brain sees life through the lizard-brain lens, then you will constantly see life through the lens of survival, competition, and comparison. If your dominant brain sees life through the monkey-brain lens, then you will constantly see life through the lens of doing whatever feels good at the moment or doing whatever your friends are doing. If, on the other hand, your dominant brain sees life through the divine-brain lens, you will have a more complete view. You can still have the benefits of the lizard-brain and the monkey-brain—*and* the divine-brain as well. Your view of life will be upward, and you will see greater possibilities in the horizon.

YOU CAN'T JUST DO THE OPPOSITE

There are some things to keep in mind when making the switch away from the strong influence of lizard-brain and monkey-brain and toward being more divinative. At times our lizard-brains take over, and we want to compete, contend (fight), or conquer. These are all lizard-brain, eat-or-be-eaten strategies. Sometimes our monkey-brains take over, and we want to compare, criticize, or complain. These are common lizard and monkey-brain tactics that occur when we are feeling bad. We simply can't go from competing, contending, and conquering to *not* competing, *not* contending, and *not* conquering. The reason we can't simply shift to the opposite of where we've been, is because we are still in the same brain. With our lizard-brain asking the question, "Can I eat it?" or "Can it eat me?" we are simply shifting from the *eating or conquering* thinking, to *getting eaten or getting conquered thinking*. When the monkey-brain says we are feeling bad, we want to tell ourselves to feel better. Either way, we are still in the monkey-brain mode of processing our world in terms of feeling good versus feeling bad.

Look back at the surfing story. You couldn't go from falling shortly after you stood up on the surfboard, to just telling myself to not fall. You need a whole new mindset. You need the surf instructor to tell you to look up and look toward the shore and above. Once you looked up and toward the shore, you could surf toward the shore for as long as you wanted. You didn't need to worry about whether you were going to fall to the left or to the right. You weren't thinking about whether you were going to fall at all. You were thinking about where you wanted to go. We need a new coach or teacher or in this case, surf instructor to show a new way to surf longer. We need the divine-brain to take over. We need the relative brightness of the sun (divine-brain) to give new light to our thinking and understanding. It's been mentioned before but it is worth repeating.

> The first decision you can make as a leader is to choose to make your divine-brain your dominant brain. All other choices and decisions will flow from this first choice.

Chapter Quiz:

The great lesson from the fairy tale *The Ugly Duckling* is that you have the power ____ ______________.

With the power to choose the greatest choice you can make is to make your ___________ brain your _____________ brain. All other choices and decisions will flow from this first choice.

CHAPTER FIVE

DISTANCE BETWEEN HEAVEN AND HELL

I mentioned earlier that I get on airplanes from time to time for work. On one particular flight as I was comfortably seated in the plane, I was watching people as they boarded the plane. One passenger in particular had an obvious look of excitement. She sat next to me and after a few moments of chit-chat, I asked her where she was coming from or headed to. She excitedly said that she had just come from a conference where she had learned what she felt was the most important lesson she had ever learned. I thought to myself, *Wow! That's quite a conference.* Curious, I asked her what lesson she had learned that was the most important. She said, "I learned the physical distance between heaven and hell."

That was quite a statement, and it made me really curious. Of course, I just had to ask, "So, how far is that?"

She said, "About twelve to eighteen inches—the distance from your head to your heart!" Heaven is when your head and your heart work together and help you realize the person and leader you have the potential to be. Hell is when your head and heart are not in synch. In other words your heart may be going in one direction and your head in a different direction.

This idea of your head and your heart working together was profound. As you ponder what she said, think about how you might apply this idea everyday of your life. One of the first things that came to mind was how many times we already get a little bit of heaven, perhaps without ever appreciating it, and the profound effect other people have on us. Think about the profound impact we have on others. In other words, do we use only our minds to notice the many things that happen to us daily—forgetting to notice with our hearts as well?

Consider the following simple acts:

- Think about friends who take the time to listen to you, understand you, and have a good sense of where you're coming from. Those friends are there for you even if it's just to talk. They don't judge. They just take the time to listen and understand. Don't you appreciate them in your heart as well as in your mind?
- Your teacher cheerfully greets you when you come in to class. He or she calls you by name. Your teacher praises you publicly when you do something great and spends one-on-one time with you to help when you struggle. Don't you appreciate your teacher and class just a bit more? Doesn't that motivate you to keep on trying?
- You go to a favorite store; the people who work there are friendly; you see familiar faces; they remember you and may even know you by name; and they genuinely want to help you. Isn't that the reason you keep going back to the same store, even if their prices aren't better than another store?
- Think of a beloved family member who sees you better than you see yourself. Think about this family member who showed you great love even when you did something dumb (we all do something dumb from time to time). Think about when she or he shared some great advice with you along with caring. Didn't you want to be the better person that family member expected you to be?

These acts stem from the heart, not just the mind. Do you and I respond in kind? What if everything we did was more than feeling like "I *have* to," but was balanced with love? What if we consciously try to be as good a listener to our friends as they are to us? What if you thanked your teachers for their kindness, for thinking about you and taking their time to help you when you struggle, and for just being good teachers? What if we acknowledged the friendly and helpful people at the store, letting them know how much we appreciate their genuine kindness and service? What if we saw each member of our family as the best person he or she *can* be even if he or she is not that person today? What difference would it make if you always thought this way as a leader? What if you and I saw all of our interactions through our hearts as well as through our minds? I'm sure you already do, many times over. As you stop and think about this, you will recognize that much of what you already do is very good. You need to celebrate every action you take when your heart and mind are in sync. You may even do this so often that you think it's not a big deal. Are you kidding me? It's a huge deal! It's a huge deal, because that distance between your head and your heart is coming closer together and you are experiencing a little bit of heaven.

Another lesson learned from this airplane passenger's excitement was her expectation. Her excitement about having her head and heart working together was more than just hope. She believed in her heart of hearts, that if her heart and mind were aligned, she would see improvement in her life, and she would be happy. Little by little she would awaken to the awesomeness that is within her.

Have you ever met people at school, maybe teachers, coaches, the bus driver, your doctor, dentist, or even the employees in a grocery store who just absolutely love what they do and are great at it? What makes them great and not just good is they know what they are doing and do it well (head), and they love what they do (heart). You have probably met other people in the exact same jobs, and have wondered how they ever got their jobs or why they wanted those jobs in the first place. They either dislike what they do, or there's no excitement behind their work. They are just doing what needs to get done, and they are miserable. This is a great lesson that is worth your time to notice. At some point you are probably going to be thinking about what you may want to do for work. As you think about different options, think about it with your head and your heart.

While some are great at what they do and others may be so-so, most people are somewhere in the middle. Most people haven't yet taken the time to figure out in their hearts and in their minds what kind of person and leader they want to be. For this reason adding this "distance between heaven and hell" as one of the core ideas to help you awaken the awesomeness that is within you is helpful.

Chapter Quiz:

According to the story in this chapter what is the distance between heaven and hell?

a) 26.2 miles
b) Twelve to eighteen inches—the distance from your head to your heart
c) Lunch to dinner

CHAPTER SIX

PRE-FORGIVENESS

THE next cool and exciting idea that would awaken the awesomeness that is in you is called pre-forgiveness. I first learned what it meant to be pre-forgiven from one of my jobs. I have been fortunate enough to have had a boss who has been a tremendous friend and professional mentor for me. His name is Chuck Farnsworth. Like all bosses do when they have a new employee, he went through the typical stuff most bosses go through on the first day. He talked about what my new job was all about and what needed to be done, what forms had to be filled out, paperwork to sign, etcetera. Then what he said next changed my view of leadership forever. He told me about his relationship with the rest of the team and what he hoped would be our relationship. He said, "You are pre-forgiven!"

I was puzzled at first and wanted him to explain what pre-forgiveness meant. He told me he was sure mistakes would be made, because we all make mistakes. He told me to remember that if and when I make those mistakes, that I was forgiven for them. I remember thinking to myself: *Is this guy for real?* At the time, I didn't know him well. Giving him the benefit of the doubt and hoping that he was genuine, I wanted to live up to my end of the bargain to be pre-forgiven. In exchange for being pre-forgiven he wanted two things. First, he wanted me to tell him about the mistakes. Second, he wanted me to tell him what I learned from my mistakes. He taught me that if all you did was confess your mistakes, it would not be very helpful. He wanted me to tell him what I learned, so the whole team could learn from my experience. Not only could the whole team learn from what people were doing well, they could also learn from the mistakes that were made.

The notion of being pre-forgiving with others is a wonderful and sacred trust. The idea of being pre-forgiven can be a bit tricky however. This is a two-edged sword. It can quickly build trust when it's done right, but it can also destroy trust quickly if not handled with care. Before you tell anyone he or she is pre-forgiven, slow down just a bit. The reason you should slow down is because before you can truly pre-forgive someone else, you need to pre-forgive yourself!

Before we go too deep into this idea of pre-forgiveness, let's talk about what pre-forgiveness means and what it is not. Pre-forgiveness is not the same as trust. Trust is something you have to earn. If you disappoint someone because you have not been worthy of their trust, there are consequences for that. For example if you come home later than you promised your parents, you might be grounded for that. Just to give another example, if you don't turn in your homework regularly and on time, as a consequence your grades may go down.

Forgiveness, on the other hand, is not something that you have to earn. Instead, pre-forgiveness is something you remember to recognize. Pre-forgiveness means remembering the awesomeness, the divine, the potential, and the very best that exists within each person. For example, I remember the very first time I held my daughter Leslie when she was first born. I remember very vividly the first time she opened her eyes and looked at me. I'll never forget that moment. When she looked at me I could see and sense and feel that she is a person with great intelligence and love. It was so awesome. Do you remember holding a little baby in your arms and being very careful because you knew babies are fragile and precious to their parents, but you also saw they are so cute and you wanted them to smile back at you when you smiled at them? Do you remember at that moment thinking: *This baby is awesome*! Well, forgiveness is remembering that feeling about people even when they make mistakes. We are all the same little babies; we just get bigger. Pre-forgiveness is a promise you make to yourself that you will remember the awesomeness in other people (and of course-yourself) before they make mistakes. They will make mistakes, because everyone makes mistakes. Unconditionally seeing someone's potential and worth is a mind-set and heart-set. (Remember the distance between heaven and hell—heart vs. head that we mentioned earlier.)

Pre-forgiving yourself means remembering your own awesomeness even when *you* make mistakes. It's so easy to get down on yourself when mistakes are made. Remember that *you* are awesome. You are a person with great worth, with great potential and a divine-brain. You are a person with unique talents, and you are capable of contributing in significant and brilliant ways. In other words, when you are able to see the divine in yourself, you can and will have the ability to see the divine in others even if their actions are motivated by monkey-brain or lizard-brain thinking. They have divine-brains, because we all do. So pre-forgiving yourself is seeing the best in you even when you do things that are not the best. We will invariably all make mistakes, and we can get derailed quickly. Learn to quickly forgive yourself in the midst of occasional mistakes, and continue to see yourself as a person of great worth, potential, and strength.

The best place to start a culture of pre-forgiveness is with *you*. Follow the process that my boss Chuck shared with me. First, confess to yourself, or in other words, have the awareness that you made a mistake. Second, take the time to really think through your mistakes and ask, "What can be learned from this?" Remember, you can choose to make your divine-brain your dominant brain, and pre-forgiveness is a divine-brain thought. You can do it. Your own perfection or completeness and full development is at stake. Persist, even when you make mistakes on occasion. We all have to practice being our own best cheerleader. Learn from the past mistakes, and don't dwell there. Keep moving forward.

Ponder for a moment what your family or circle of friends or school would be like if everyone were pre-forgiving. What would you anticipate would be different in a family or friends or school environment that was pre-forgiving compared to one that was not? Jot down a few ideas.

____

____

____

____

____

____

____

____

Go the other way. What if in your family or school people did not feel like they were pre-forgiven, but instead they felt like they were pre-punished? Life is tough enough as it is without feeling that you have to defend yourself from people who are supposed to be your friends, allies, and people who are supposed to have your back. What would your family or school or friends be like if people felt pre-punished or pre-judged?

> You, yourself, as much as anybody in the entire universe, deserve your love and affection.
>
> —Buddha

CHAPTER SEVEN

THE WEAVE OF LIFE: "TO-BE" and "TO-DO"

WOW! We have covered quite a bit in just a few pages. Ponder all of that information and let it soak in. You can probably tell this is not one of those books that you read quickly, even though it's not very big. It's the kind of book you read and re-read and think about. The topic of leadership is so important because it impacts every part of our lives. If you could look at leadership at its simplest form, it would be this: consider a pair of jeans you wear regularly. If you look closely at the fabric of your jeans, chances are they have been woven. Look at leadership from a weaving metaphor.

When weaving in a loom, there are rows of thread that are placed up and down or vertically in the loom. These rows of thread are collectively called the *warp*. The collective width of these vertical rows or warp determines the width of the jeans fabric. Each row of jean thread that will make up the warp has to be strong enough to withstand being stretched and placed under tension. It's important to note that it takes a great deal of effort just to get the warp set up, before the rest of the jeans can be woven. The jean material that crisscrosses at right angles or perpendicular to the warp material to create your jeans is called the *weft*. The warp and the weft are equally important for the strength and integrity of the jeans. The warp and weft complement each other. Without one or the other, the jeans will unravel, and you will be left with just a lump of jean thread. If the warp and weft are properly woven, they can form a strong and beautiful fabric.

As we apply this metaphor to leadership, the weft (the material that is used second) represents all the activities or to-do's that is part of being a great leader. As we move further in this book you will have a series of to-do's to choose from. Have you ever written down a to-do list? We're going to talk about coming up with your leadership to-do list. Having your to-do list, however, is not enough. In our weaving metaphor, the warp (set up first) represents our to-be list or those things we deliberately pay attention to in order to develop our character of leadership. Just as the warp gives the jean fabric its strength and has to be set up first, so our character gives our lives strength and has to be set up first. Character is the foundation for leadership. Just as your jean fabric can wear out quicker and unravel if the warp is not strong enough, so can our ability to lead and live our lives unravel if we don't give our character enough of our time to set up properly, to focus sufficiently and develop fully.

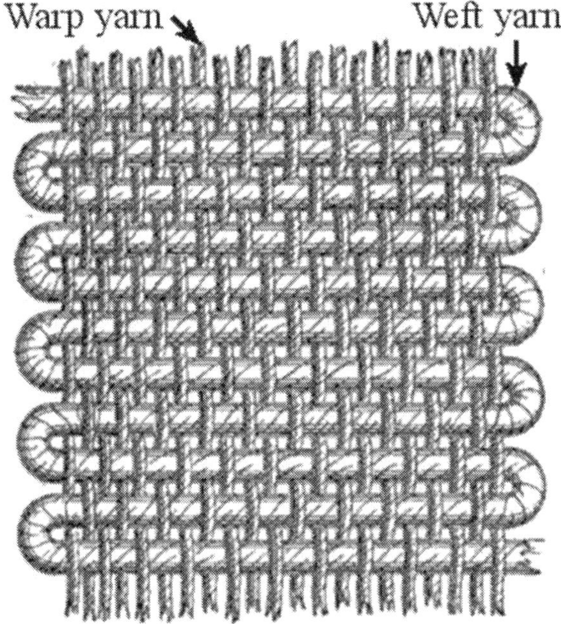

> Character is that which reveals moral purpose, exposing the class of things a man chooses and avoids.
>
> —Aristotle

Think for a moment about the lives of the so-called famous and successful people whose fame, fortune, and success are replaced with scandal, lost fortunes, damaged reputations, and broken families, because their character has been compromised or it was weak from the start. Of course these stories are not limited to those we see in the news, but they can impact you and me just the same. Our lives can also unravel if we don't give sufficient focus to developing our character (our to-be list) as well as achieving goals and completing our to-do lists. Sometimes there is so much focus on all the stuff we have to do and finishing our to-do list that we're becoming human doings. Remember you are not a human *doing* but a human *being!* You are an awesome human being with divine potential. As you learn about leadership, remember that your to-be list is just as important as your to-do list.

Chapter Quiz:

The vertical threads in a loom are called the ______________
and represent our ______________list.

The horizontal threads in a loom are called the ______________
and represent our ________________list.

We are not human doings but human ______________.

CHAPTER EIGHT

ALLEGORY #1: ALLEGORY OF THE TREES

WE have just gone through five ideas that will help to awaken the awesomeness that is in you. Now we'll cover the second set of concepts we mentioned. These will be covered through allegories. The first allegory is the allegory of the trees.

The world's oldest continually-standing tree is the Bristlecone Pine, living nearly five thousand years, and having grown to about 60 feet high. The Redwood tree on the other hand, can reach over 300 feet in height and can live more than two thousand years. When we study these trees a little closer we learn other interesting things that can teach us some very valuable lessons.

The Bristlecone lives where practically nothing else can. The Bristlecone Pine is almost always found in elevations above 10,000 feet in the windy mountaintops in the western portion of the United States. The growing season is a short six weeks, and it rains less than a foot per year. Less than a foot of rain per year is the definition of desert conditions. This desert condition, where these trees thrive, is one of the driest places on earth in the summer and is very cold in the winter.

The Redwood trees, on the other hand, live in a mild, moist climate in the coastal northwest part of California. The Redwood trees receive an average of 70 inches of rain per year. The soil is rich. There is infrequent frost where these Redwood trees thrive, and it snows very little.

The oldest Bristlecone Pines live in the most exposed sites, with a considerable amount of space between each tree. Not only is there space between each tree, but the Bristlecone is also isolated because few other species can survive the rugged conditions. The Bristlecone roots sink wide and deep into the rocky soil. The Redwood trees, on the other hand, grow close together with other Redwood trees, and their roots are shallow and interwoven.

What a contrast between the Bristlecone and Redwood trees. Despite their differences, they both live such a long time. Perhaps you can see the similarities and parallels between these trees and your own life or the lives of your family members, friends, neighbors, or kids at school. As you could imagine some of them come from ideal conditions, as does the Redwood tree. Other people however, may come from tough harsh conditions like the Bristlecone Pine. Have you noticed that some people seem to have everything you can imagine? Maybe intertwined roots could be a metaphor for being part of an ideal, supportive, and loving family and extended family, while someone else may come from broken homes. Maybe mild conditions and rich soil is a metaphor for living in the best neighborhood and the best school with the best teachers and great friends. Someone else, on the other hand, may come from violent neighborhoods, not the best teachers and schools—and true friends may be scarce. Maybe plenty of rain represents many opportunities to grow that are readily available, while little rain or desert conditions is a metaphor for lack of growth opportunities. Regardless, you probably know people from both extremes who manage to live wonderful lives and are sources of inspiration for all of us. How can people, like these trees, have such different backgrounds, yet, regardless of their backgrounds, become the people they want to be?

Redwood Tree	**Bristlecone Pine**
Grows 300 feet tall or more	Grows 50–60 feet tall
Coast of California	Mountains over 10,000 feet
70 inches of rain	10–12 inches of rain, desert
Grows in rich soil	Grows in rocky soil
Roots intertwine	Singular trees
Mild Conditions	Harsh, Rugged Conditions
2000 years old	Almost 5000 years old

Most of us, on the other hand, are probably somewhere in the middle. We may not have all the support and opportunities and ideal conditions we can imagine but we have more than most. Regardless of our conditions, best, worst or somewhere in the middle, the point is we can flourish and grow and be great for a long time like the Redwood tree and Bristlecone pine.

Let's look again at the Bristlecone and Redwood trees for more insights. A big reason why these trees live so long is because of their ability to fight fires from without and disease from within. Many trees live to be a few hundred years old. Again, the age of most trees are measured in hundreds not thousands of years. Fire and disease are the main reasons why other trees don't survive as long as the Bristlecone and Redwood. Bacteria, fungus, or insects prey upon most trees. However, the Bristlecone tree has a dense and highly resinous wood that acts as a barrier to insects and bacteria. The dry air in the region helps to preserve the trees from rotting.

The Redwood tree fights against disease differently. The bark of the Redwood tree may be over a foot thick and contains tannin, which protects the tree from insects, fungus, and disease. There is no insect that can kill a Redwood tree. Both of these trees have the ability to fight attacks from within because of the makeup of the trees themselves.

As far as fighting fires, many other trees have falling leaves that can act as fuel in the event of a lightning strike. Combined with having a dense forest, fires can spread quickly from one tree to the next. This is not the case with the Bristlecone Pine. First of all, the Bristlecone needles last so long they don't create a fuel source to be burned in the event of a fire. Not only that, but because of the conditions due to the rocky soil, harsh windy environment with little rainfall, there are not too many other plants that live around the Bristlecone Pine. Because of this, in the event of a lightning strike, fires can't spread. The Redwood tree, on the other hand, fights fires with its thick spongy bark that contains materials with similar chemical make-up as those used today in fire extinguishers.

Whether it's these trees striving for longevity, or us trying to become the people and leaders we want to be, both requires dealing with our own personal fires from without and our personal disease from within. It requires that our very character be resistant against those things that tempt us to compromise the integrity of our character. The very word *disease* means "without ease." So, living with integrity or living according to our chosen beliefs, values and standards (remember the word *standards* from our definition of leadership) gives us peace; otherwise we live without ease. Fighting our personal fires from without requires having a barrier of protection thick enough to withstand tremendous heat, like the Redwood tree, or we must put ourselves in an environment where fires can't spread or intensify, like the Bristlecone Pine.

It is interesting to note that with some Redwood trees, you will see the trees hollowed out. Maybe you have seen pictures of redwood trees so hollowed out that a car can be driven through the middle of the tree. They are sometimes referred to as chimney trees. Cracks or spaces in the bark contribute to these Redwood trees being hollowed out. Although the bark itself is thick, over time, fires attack the Redwood trees through these openings. The more the trees are hollowed out through many fires over the centuries, the weaker the tree becomes, and the Redwood tree strains to hold its tremendous bulk, eventually crumbling under its own weight. As we have learned from the Redwood chimney tree, we need to guard against those little cracks and openings where fires from without can attack. We need to be equally careful with the big and small activities over time that would detract us from being the type of people and leaders we want to be. This will take time and more especially, practice and persistence.

PRAYER AND MEDITATION

We mentioned that both the Bristlecone Pines and Redwood trees fight disease from within by the very make-up of the tree. So how do we create this barrier of protection from personal fires from without and personal dis-ease from within, which rob us of our leadership potential, to live according to the standards that we are inspired to live?

> We need to dedicate a portion of our time every day to strengthening our divine-brains.

How do we do this? Recall the lesson from our three-part brains and *The Ugly Duckling* that we have the power to decide that our divine-brains will dominate our thinking instead of our lizard-brains or monkey-brains. This is the first great decision we need to make— that we can make a deliberate choice to have our divine-brains dominate our thoughts and harness our power to choose.

Consider the poem "Invictus" from William Ernest Henley that celebrates this power that exists in us.

Invictus

Out of the night that covers me,
Black as the Pit from pole to pole,
I thank whatever gods may be
For my unconquerable soul.
In the fell clutch of circumstance
I have not winced nor cried aloud.
Under the bludgeoning of chance
My head is bloody, but unbowed.
Beyond this place of wrath and tears
Looms but the Horror of the shade,
And yet the menace of the years
Finds, and shall find me, unafraid.
It matters not how strait the gate,
How charged with punishments the scroll,
I am the master of my fate:
I am the captain of my soul.

This is a wonderful poem that arouses in mankind the ability to realize his/her potential. As you consider your history classes at school, look at how mankind has improved over the centuries and how that improvement is accelerated year after year. It is simply awesome. We are all so fortunate that enough people have made the huge decision to mentally and emotionally (remember the distance between heaven and hell—head to heart) tap into their divine-brains. We have all benefited from these advancements.

Despite having this strong sense that we are the masters of our fates and the captains of our souls (I personally believe this is so) we also know that our abilities and courage have their limitations. The ability to recognize this limitation and to have the humility to act on these limitations can be one of our greatest strengths. For within all of us is also a voice that says there is a greater source of power higher than our own. We all have the ability and opportunity to consistently tap into spiritual strength or our source for meaning. For some, spiritual strength means religion, while for others it may come from nature, science, literature, music, art, and so forth. Because by some estimates over 80 percent of everyone worldwide is affiliated with a religious group, let me give the context of spiritual strength through the lens of religion.

The second great decision we can make, besides deciding that our divine-brains will be our dominant brains, is to start and end each day using our divine-brains. Being who we are or hope to be depends on which brain is allowed to be most dominant and which brain is most used.

Praying or connecting to your source of meaning through meditation is a powerful use of your time when it is done as the first activity of the morning and the last activity at night. The world around us is a competitive and complex place where survival and conquest (lizard-brain), emotions, and fitting in (monkey-brain) can dominate our time, thoughts, feelings, and action's. When we don't begin our days by praying or connecting to our sense of meaning, the lizard-brain and monkey-brain activities that surround our world begin to grab for our attention. If we do not make a conscious decision to begin and end the day with *divine-brain* type thinking, we will be drawn to the lizard-brain and monkey-brain type thinking by default.

> Prayer is not an old woman's idle amusement. If properly understood and applied, it is the most potent instrument of action.
>
> —Mahatma Gandhi

Consistent prayer and connecting to a higher sense of purpose increases our capacity and ability to use our divine-brains in the hard moments. Think back to a time when you regretted doing or saying something. They need not be huge regrets, just the little ones. Perhaps you got impatient and said unkind things to a friend or family member. Perhaps in a moment of anger you acted inappropriately. For most of us, these regrettable moments happened when our lizard-brains or monkey-brains dominated our thinking. We wish we had the moments back and hope that our very best divine-brains would have made better decisions or found better words.

Consistent daily morning and evening prayer or connection to meaning through meditation build our reservoir of strength in those tough moments. What should you pray for and meditate about? Begin each morning by reviewing those things for which you are genuinely grateful. Although not everything is ideal in every way, going through this "gratitude attitude" exercise will help all of us realize how blessed we are in all things. Be grateful for the natural beauties you have around you every day, and pray to have eyes to see them. We have family members, friends, neighbors, and other relationships that give us strength and hope. Be grateful for friends and family who love us and whom we love. We have physical conveniences and technological advances that kings, pharaohs, and rulers of days past could only have dreamt of. In the history of the world how many people have had a cell phone, computers, cars, microwave oven, lighting in their homes with the flip of a switch? Even things like central heat, central air, running water, a stove are great conveniences we take for granted. Review and be grateful for your belief system and how it has blessed your life. Review and be grateful for your unique talents. Be grateful for challenges that help you grow and develop your character. Be grateful for life itself and for the freedoms you enjoy. As you go through this simple exercise, can't you just feel you're your awareness expanding? What are you grateful for? Make a quick list.

____

____

____

After you are done expressing gratitude for all of things you are fortunate to have, be and do, follow that thought by thinking of how you can improve yourself as well as lift others today, in your home, at school, with your friends, and in all areas of your life. Pray for the courage to live according to the person and leader you want to be and for the strength of character you want to have. Before you go to bed, review how you have lifted others that day. Celebrate your courageous efforts to live according to your standards in both the big and little things. This daily and nightly accountability system will remind you to keep your divine-brain as your dominant brain. Your divine-brain will also help you make the adjustments you need to make to realize the person and leader you want to be. Add to this the habit of daily reading of scriptures or inspiring literature. The lessons you learn from your reading will also help you keep your divine-brain as your dominant brain. As you make these simple activities habits, you will notice that you are changing as a person and leader. Your very nature will change, and you will recognize that you are indeed divine.

ZIGZAG PATH TO GROWTH

When we examined the Redwood tree and Bristlecone Pines, we explored primarily their protection from fire and disease, which helped them to achieve longevity. Let's shift from protection to actual growth. If prayer and meditation along with reading scriptures and inspiring literature is my focus at the beginning and ending of each day, what should be my focus in between? What does it take for us to awaken the awesomeness of our potential and continue to grow and lead lives of fulfillment and contribution? First, let's take a look at how growth occurs and what may restrain our progress. Let's go back to the monkey-brain for a moment. Remember that part of the monkey-brain says that it is more desirable to feel good than to not feel good. This mammalian part of our brains (or monkey-brain) tells us that we would rather avoid pain and move towards repeating pleasure.

So in the following continuum, given the choice between the far left side where we don't feel so good or we feel pain, compared to moving to the extreme right where we feel good or we feel pleasure, nearly everyone would likely prefer moving to the far right. In our Zigzag Path to Growth this continuum will be our X-axis. The Y-axis of this model represents our growth and contribution. Growth and contribution refers to our personal growth and contributing our unique talents and abilities for the benefit of others. Together they are a big part of our life's mission. There is a voice within each of us that says, "You are wonderful. You are a person of great worth. You have unique talents and insights that can contribute and benefit others in significant ways." Moving further up the Y-axis represents higher levels of growth and contribution towards our life's unique mission. Let's put these two together. When we have achieved high growth and contribution, and we also feel great, then we are achieving our mission—our sense of "being."

Figure 1: **DESIRED GROWTH PATH**

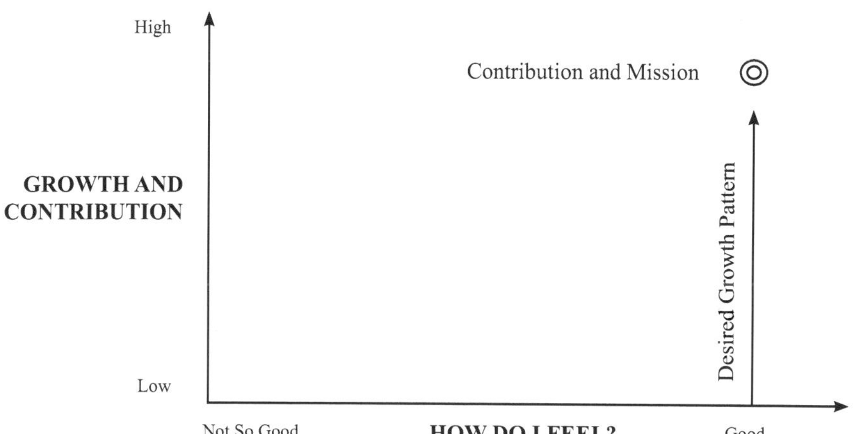

Of course, we all wish that we could feel good all of the time while growing and living a life that is fulfilling for ourselves as we contribute to our loved ones and the rest of humanity—and live happily ever after. That is the kind of life that is represented in the graph above. Unfortunately, it doesn't work that way, and our experiences verify it as well.

Figure 2: **TYPICAL GROWTH PATH**

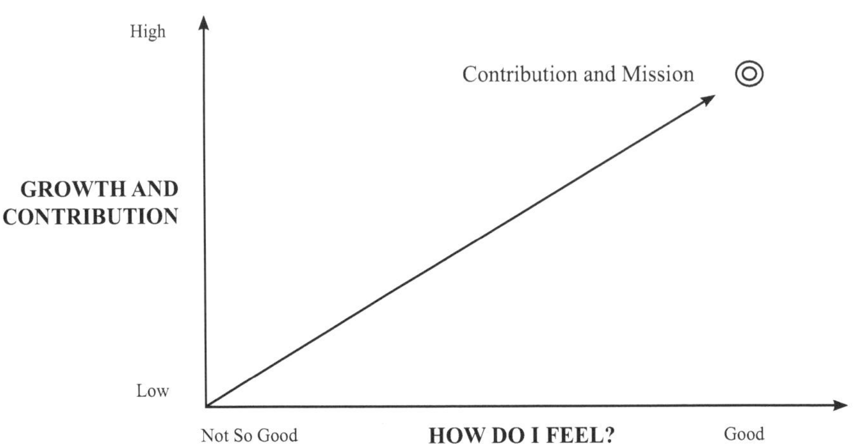

This Figure 2 graph is a simple representation of how our growth more typically occurs. Think back to when you were learning how to ride a bike. Remember going through that experience, being scared and maybe even terrified. In other words, on the X-axis of how you were feeling, you were on the far left. As far as your growth when it comes to riding a bike, you were at the bottom. Perhaps you could hardly put your feet on the pedals, because you kept stretching your legs out, anticipating and bracing yourself for when you would tilt too far to the left or to the right, and perhaps fall. The more you practiced, however, the better you felt, and you were also growing and improving your bike-riding skills. In other words, you were moving further to the right as well as further up on this diagonal line. Once you understood how to ride a bike, you were having fun and feeling good. It's the same bike, and you are the same person, but the change in how you felt was a result of your confidence, growth, and development. Think of other times when you have gone through a similar growth experience whether at school, at home, or learning a new skill.

MATH HOMEWORK

I could just as easily have chosen any school subject, but I'll use math as an example, because this is what happened in our home. Our son Benjamin has always been a hard worker when it comes to school. He is a good student and does well on all of his school subjects. But on one particular day, when he was eight years old, he'd had enough of math. He couldn't understand the concepts, and he just sat there and cried. Over and over he would say, "I hate math. I hate math. I hate math." Every now and then he would insert, "Math is stupid. Math is stupid." My eleven-year son, Spencer, glanced over at his distraught brother, looked at Ben's homework, and said, "Are you kidding me? My math homework is harder than your homework. I wish I had your math homework!" Let me graph how our continual individual growth typically occurs over time.

Figure 3: **ZIGZAG PATH TO GROWTH FOR SPENCER AND BEN**

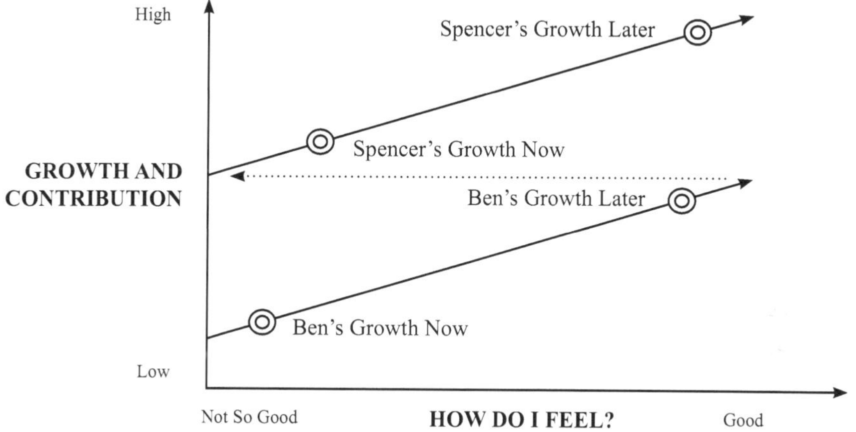

Ben is in the stage in his understanding of his math homework where he doesn't feel good and understands little of the math he has been assigned to complete. The more he studies, however, the more he'll understand it, and the better he'll feel. Like my bike example, he will move up and to the right of the diagonal line of the Zigzag Path to Growth. When he moves to the top of the diagonal line, all will be well in the Fonbuena household ... at least for a while.

Here comes the tricky part of the Zigzag Path to Growth. Just when Ben is beginning to understand the current math problems and feeling good about school and math, he'll be introduced to another new concept that he won't understand, and he won't feel so good in the beginning. And so the process is repeated as he progresses through basic math, to algebra, then eventually on to calculus and beyond. As he moves up the "growth and contribution" continuum, he will zig and zag through the "how do you feel" continuum. Spencer has to go through the same process. Spencer just happens to be further up on the growth and contribution continuum. So Ben and I decided to put down the math for a while, and we just talked about this Zigzag Path to Growth. I told Ben that math will get better, and the difficulty he is experiencing now won't last forever. I assured him that it won't be long before he thinks the problems he struggles with now will be really easy. He felt a whole lot better when this was explained to him.

However, we also discussed that that as he progresses through math, he will go through the process all over again. All of a sudden he looked a bit depressed. Can you blame him? Think back to the monkey-brain. In essence, my message to him was, we are going to do everything possible to help him feel better, and then we are going to make a deliberate decision to ask him to do something that does not feel good, just when he is feeling comfortable and celebrating success. If I were him I'd be thinking, "Are you crazy? Why would you do something that is harder and doesn't feel good when doing something easier and feels better is an option? Good question. My answer to this puzzle would be, "Feeling good is not our only criteria." Personal growth, character development, living according to your life's unique mission and contribution are also important, and in the long run, these improvements are our goal.

He just looked at me as if to say, "Can I talk to Mommy?" It was obvious he wasn't convinced. We discussed that in those tough moments, both Mommy and I would help him. He didn't seem to mind the concept of going through hard moments so long as he wasn't going to go through them alone. He stopped crying, got up off the couch, and with a new resolve started working on the math homework again. Like my son Ben, most of us would be willing to go through tough moments and eventually get to growth and contribution, so long as we know we won't go through them alone. Otherwise our monkey-brains wonder whether it's worth the pain, and our lizard-brains wonder whether we are going to get eaten in the process.

Let me just insert a couple of side notes here. There are times when we go through growth at a high level as well as at a steep incline, and we enjoy every moment of it. For example, we have a neighbor whose daughter can't wait to get to school every day. She takes the most difficult classes and just *loves* the challenge of learning. Then she comes home and can't wait to share what she learned, even though no one is interested in listening. She just loves learning. I have a friend who loves to exercise and looks forward to the hard moments of a workout. For these people the growing pains still exist; they have just adjusted to it and have put more emphasis and focus on the growth that will come from their growing pain and less on the growing pain itself. For most of us, however, we do feel the growing pains are ... well ... *painful* and it takes more of an effort. We could all wish it were easier, but mostly it's not. Once in a blue moon it is easier, and we're grateful for those times when they happen. Either way, we know that there is no getting around the growing pain. There is only going through it. The more we realize that it is a normal part of our growth process, the better we handle the growing pain.

It's worth mentioning a side note about the growing pains. We're not referring to enjoying pain for its own sake, where we stay there in the name of growth. No. I'm interested in growth and fulfillment and the joy that comes from it. If some growing pain is required and such pain is normal, then I'm fine with it—only to the extent necessary—but pain for pain's sake is not sustainable or healthy.

As you look at Figure 3 Zigzag Path to Growth somewhere along this journey, chances are, mistakes are going to be made. You have never met a person who has never made a mistake at school, never made a mistake at home, or never made a mistake ever. Mistakes happen. This is where pre-forgiveness comes in. Pre-forgive yourself and keep going up this Zigzag Path to Growth. This path to growth will always be the case even long after you are retired from being a teenager. There is a successful executive who was asked in the prime of the company's success his secret to the company's achievement. His quick reply was, "Double your failure rate."

> In your journey to growth, tough times won't last forever and good times shouldn't.
>
> --Charles Fonbuena

Remember in chapter seven, we used the weaving metaphor, where we wanted to develop in the fabric of our lives, the warp of character, and the weft of goals and activities? The growing pain we have been examining in our

Zigzag Path to Growth coincides with character development. The more we persist and persevere through the growing pains, the stronger our character becomes as we are stretched.

> Character cannot be developed in ease and quiet. Only through experience of trial and suffering can the soul be strengthened, ambition inspired, and success achieved.
>
> —Helen Keller

Look at the individual Zigzag Path to Growth another way as illustrated in Figure 4. With each cycle up the Zigzag Path to Growth, we first go through growing pain. Deep down we know this, and simply acknowledging this reality is half the battle. The other half of the battle of solving this equation is simply going through the growing pains and realizing and remembering that the growing pain won't last forever. It may feel like forever, but there is always an end. There is no going around, but only through. When we persist and endure, at some point we'll move up the growth and fulfillment axis as we gain more expertise, and we'll move further right on the "feel good" axis as our confidence increases.

Figure 4: **ZIGZAG PATH TO GROWTH**

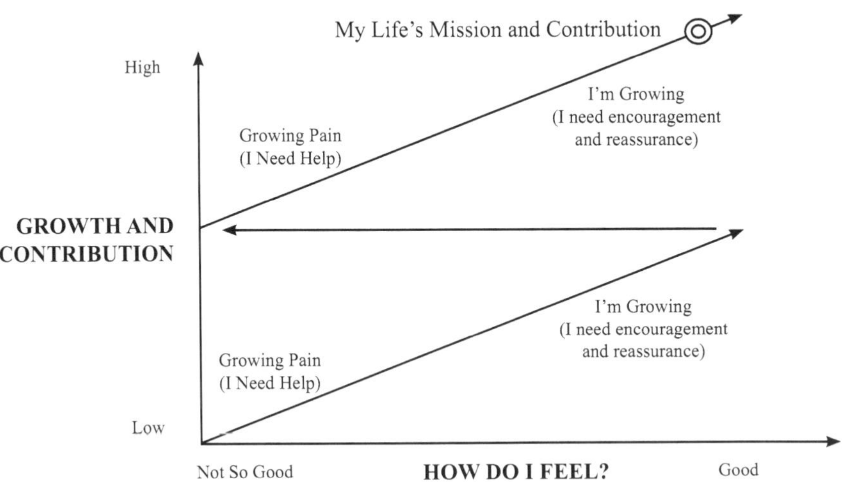

The toughest part is the growing pains area, and this can be made so much easier if there is someone there to help us. We would rather not do this alone. Our monkey-brains, which prefer pleasure over pain, will surely continue to remind us to get help or get out. When I mention getting help, it doesn't mean someone will take the growing pain away from us. That would defeat the purpose and only encourage us to be dependent on somebody else. I'm talking about getting the kind of help beyond our current abilities. For example, my son Ben didn't understand his math homework, and no amount of persistence or positive mental attitude would have made a difference. He needed help, because it was simply beyond his current understanding at that time. Like Ben, most of the time, we don't need a lot of help. We just need a little bit of help at critical times in critical areas.

Think of specific people who have been there for you in your moments of growing pains. They were life savers. Of course the more we realize and appreciate how important help from others is in these critical times, the more we'll feel and understand where others are coming from, and we'll realize the need to help others in their "growing pains" moments. We generally appreciate giving and receiving help in equal measure. Once we get past the toughest part of the growing pains, then what we need is encouragement. We long to have and will appreciate the reassurance that we are on the right path, and we need to simply stay the course. We're grateful for those who help us quiet our inner doubts and fears that creep in from time to time in our journey to success. Once you achieve and celebrate your successes, you can only linger for so long before the voice inside of you longing to "be" the person and leader you want to be says, "Let's take another trip up the Zigzag Path to Growth to the next level."

> Don't wish things were easier, wish you were better.
>
> —Author Unknown

When you look at the longevity of the Redwood trees and Bristlecone Pines, you can be grateful for the lessons they teach. As you see people consistently and persistently apply the individual Zigzag Path to Growth, their natures are changed. They see the growing pains as part of the process. They worry less, because they recognize that hard times won't last forever, and in the end they know they will grow and be better. They anticipate the growth opportunities and the accompanying growing pains that will surely come again, and they recognize that with each successive cycle through the Zigzag Path to Growth, their courage, resolve, and character is stretched and strengthened. Their capacities and abilities are improved and magnified. Remember the warp and weft metaphor. At the top of each growth cycle they take the time to celebrate getting to the top of their climb. You can be a great leader whether you come from ideal conditions like the Redwood trees or harsh conditions like the Bristlecone Pines.

Chapter Quiz:

How do the redwood tree and bristlecone pine fight fires?

How do the redwood tree and bristlecone pine fight disease?

To help your divine-brain become your dominant brain, what could you do first thing in the morning and last thing at night?

As you move up the Zigzag Path to Growth, growing pains are just part of the process. True or False

CHAPTER NINE

ALLEGORY #2: OXEN PULL

FOR thousands of years before the invention of tractors and other farm machinery, oxen have been yoked together and used to pull out tree stumps to clear a field, to plow, and to do other work on farms. The oxen were an integral part of life for many farmers whose livelihood depended on the oxen for the heavy burdens of farming. Today the contribution of the oxen is celebrated with oxen-pull contests in different parts of the world. Two oxen, yoked together are hitched to a sled, and they pull the sled for a designated distance. All of the oxen teams that can pull the sled will move on to the next round. With each round, weight is added to the sled. The team that can pull the most weight wins.

Much like the oxen-pull contest, each of us goes through life with our own unique loads we must pull. From time to time, weight is added. Sometimes life asks us to carry a load that is temporary, like a hard class, and other times life asks us to carry more permanent loads like our personal weaknesses. Too often we try to pull our loads all by ourselves. It's more difficult that way. We may even succeed from time to time, but with each successive addition of weight, the difficulty feels more like multiplication. We'll eventually need help. The oxen, when working together, can pull more than the sum of what they can each pull separately. Similarly, we can do more when working with others. Although the allegory of the Bristlecone Pine and Redwood trees reminds us of what we can do individually to be the leaders and people we want to be, the allegory of the oxen pull counsels us that there is a limit to what we can do alone. We need other people, and other people need us.

Interestingly, in these oxen-pull contests, the farmers try to find the best combination that would give them the highest probability of winning. The winning combination for the oxen pull involves first, the strength and training of each ox, and second, the oxen team's ability and willingness to work together. It is possible to yoke a trained and an untrained ox together with the hope that in time, the untrained ox will learn from the trained one. This takes time and could work eventually, but you wouldn't want to begin the training process during the contest. The same would hold true when it comes to teamwork. It takes time to create great teamwork. In the oxen-pull competition, a smaller pair of oxen, when contributing to each other's strengths and working perfectly in unison, can pull more than larger teams not working in partnership.

Individual Character Strength

Let's take a look at the parallels between the oxen pull and our own lives. First is the importance of individual strength. The reason we mentioned the allegory of the tree using the Redwood tree and the Bristlecone Pine is to highlight the need for individual strength. The greatest reason we want to have sufficient individual strength is to have the confidence and preparation to work with others and create a multiplying effect as an end result. As a person's individual strength increases they become more and more independent. Isn't independence one of the major goals of being a teenager? Yes and no. Yes, independence is one of the goals but not the only goal. In fact independence is just preparation for something greater, something more—the power of teams. Independence and individual strength is the foundation for teamwork. There's no other way around it. For example, have you ever been in a school team like sports, music, or even teams in class where some members of the team are more concerned about themselves than the team?

Many times the reason they act that way is because they don't have enough individual strength or they might be strong enough but they don't understand the power of teams. When teamwork is required, and a member of the team knows deep down that she is not prepared to effectively contribute to the team, she resorts to her own personal agenda to try and compensate for her lack of preparation or lack of strength of character. Individual strength is the foundation for strong teams.

We Need to Work With Others

Another parallel between the oxen pull and our own lives is the importance of seeing the value of working with others. It is interesting that most countries celebrate Independence Day. Independence is a great achievement. We also celebrate independence when we graduate, or get a driver's license. Yet, we celebrate less frequently or at least more quietly, the times when we work with others to produce wonderful results. I'm not aware of any national holidays called "Teamwork Day" or "Collaboration Day." Usually, however, most of us spend the majority of our time working and interacting with others. We need to celebrate the opportunity and privilege we have to work with others. Just as we set goals to be independent, we also need to set goals to work effectively in teams. Of course, sometimes certain people simply drive us crazy, but seen through a different mind-set and heart-set (remember that heart and mind combination again) we'll have an appreciation for what others can add to our lives and feel it an honor to lift and help others.

Being a teenager today is much more complex than being a teenager in any other time in history. We are now in a global economy which means you will be competing for jobs not just with your peers close to where you live but with others throughout the world. This implies you are, *even now,* competing with other students throughout the world not just with neighboring schools by how you prepare. Part of being prepared for a global economy is to know and practice how to work with others.

Using the oxen-pull analogy, there is more weight to pull on the sled as a result of the complexities of life in the 21st century than ever before. Independence and individual strength may be a first step, but it is no longer sufficient to meet the demands of your fast-paced and ever-changing world. Independence is only intended to be the first step. Working with others is not just good idea, but a necessary one.

Charcoal Briquettes

> In everyone's life, at some time, our inner fire goes out. It is then burst into flame by an encounter with another human being. We should all be thankful for those people who rekindle the inner spirit.
>
> —Albert Schweitzer

Look at charcoal gathered together in a barbeque as a metaphor for the importance of working with others. When the charcoal briquettes are gathered together they produce more intense heat, and the charcoals are red hot. If you separate one charcoal from the rest, it quickly cools. Of course, you can fan the single charcoal to maintain the heat, but it would take tremendous effort just to come close to the level of heat it had before you separated it from the other charcoal. Now put the same charcoal back in the middle of the coals again, and you will notice it will quickly regain the red-hot glow without much effort. Similarly, we would do better when working with others effectively than trying to do everything alone.

What Is All That Noise?

At the start of the oxen pull, the team will start to pull at the command of the trainer. Consider for a moment, the amount of noise that exists in these oxen-pull events. There is the noise that comes from other teams and trainers. There is the noise that comes from the spectators with their ooh's and aah's. There are the noises that come from different distances. The noises themselves are all different. The oxen team, however, cuts through all the noise and listens for the voice of the trainer—no one else. The trainer's voice is near, clear, and familiar. The teams are familiar with the voice of the trainer through consistent training and practice. Just as the oxen team has a trainer, as leaders, we also need a trainer whose voice will be familiar, clear, and near to us. It is easy to hear the voice of a trainer if everything else is quiet. The question is whether or not we have each paid the price to recognize the voice of that trainer, can hear the voice clearly—even when there are other voices around—and most importantly, whether we will listen to and follow the trainer's voice. Before we look at choosing a trainer, let's take a look at the other voices that may get us confused.

Other Voices

There are so many voices in the world, each trying to get our attention. The voices around us are not just varied, but unrelenting. As we choose to listen to the voice of character, remember to listen to them more often than we listen to other voices. Let's take a look at nature of the voices around us by looking at two voices in particular—television and advertising.

I remember in high school one of my classmates was writing about aliens from a far-away galaxy. These aliens sent spies to the earth to figure out what types of creatures the earthlings were. After careful observation, the alien spies went to their leader and reported that the earthlings were highly religious and devout creatures. The leader wanted to know what lead them to this conclusion. The alien spies reported the following:

- Earthlings lived in homes where there was a room dedicated just for their religious service.
- The earthlings organized their furniture so that everyone could have a good view of this object of worship.
- There were times when friends and other family members would come over just to worship this object together. After friends and family were done worshipping, they would leave.
- The earthlings worshipped this object during mealtimes. When it wasn't mealtime, the earthlings brought in food between meals, so they would not get hungry during their worship of this object.
- The spies also said that some of the earthlings worshipped this object every night.
- The children worshipped after school, on Saturdays, and first thing in the morning.
- The rest of the family would take turns worshipping on the weekend.
- There were even times when just the men worshipped this object, and they seemed to get very excited from time to time during worship.
- Everyone seemed to always be very attentive, and there was little talking.

As you have figured out by now, the alien spies concluded that the center of worship was the television.

There is nothing inherently wrong with television. TV can contribute good information and entertainment to our lives. This is, however, an example of what can happen, when we don't choose carefully and deliberately the voices we listen to. It is so easy to get distracted with enticing voices that would take us off our course. Let's go back to the oxen-pull allegory for a moment. Over time and after a great deal of practice, the oxen team can learn to recognize and follow the trainer's voice above all the other noise. The wrong voice has the same effect. If we were to listen to the wrong voice over time and with great frequency, we would follow bad advice and move away from progressing toward becoming the leader and the kind of people we want to be.

Consider the following question for a moment. How long you can you endure before you feel an absolute urge and need to turn on the television, listen to the car radio or your portable music player, surf the Internet, play a computer game, or check the e-mail , text, or social network just one more time, just in case? Most people couldn't make it for a day. If, however, you can resist for an extended period of time, congratulations! Really! You know that pulling off such a feat requires being able to listen to your inner voice long enough that you can block out the other noise. A friend of mine once made an off-the-cuff comment about listening to his music while running a marathon. He said, "I couldn't be alone with just my thoughts for the length of a marathon." It's interesting how we can be so familiar with the noise and other voices around us, yet we can be unfamiliar and maybe even uncomfortable with our own inner voice.

Unrelenting Voices

How do they do it? How has the popular media crept into our lives to the point that we don't even recognize their grasp until we try to break free—and only then do we discover how difficult it is to escape? It is nearly impossible to go through a typical day and not get inundated with advertising from the radio, television, Internet, mail, billboards, and the products themselves. The advertising done today is more clever, ubiquitous (everywhere all the time), and consistent. Conduct your own investigation, and the next time you watch a show for a complete hour, figure out how much time is spent on commercials. According to some estimates, in the 1960s there were about nine minutes of commercials for every hour of shows or programs. Nine minutes! Now, there could be as much as eighteen minutes of commercials. Eighteen minutes! The length of the commercials has been shortened from about a minute in the 1960s to less than thirty seconds in many cases currently. This means that not only are you spending twice as much time watching commercials per hour, but you are also watching the commercials from as many as four times more companies in a given hour of programming. Advertising is an unrelenting voice.

Choosing the voice you will listen to is very serious business. We cannot be casual or haphazard in our approach. Businesses and other organizations take the voice *they* want us to listen to very seriously. If we are casual about the voices we listen to, we might jeopardize our progress toward being the leaders and the people we want to be.

CHOOSING YOUR TRAINER

In this allegory of the oxen pull, the importance of the voice of the trainer cannot be overstated. If the winning combination of the oxen pull is individual strength and teamwork, the voice of the trainer affects both. After this big set up, what is the voice of the trainer? In a word--Character!

> The formation of one's character ought to be everyone's chief aim.
>
> —Johann Wolfgang von Goethe

I believe the reason why character should be everyone's aim is because it helps us get closer to being the type of leader we want to be. Persist in your quest to be the leader that lives by a chosen set of standards. Persist even though you may make mistakes. There is a legend and a phrase called the Persian flaw. The legend says that in ancient times, the rug makers in Persia were a deeply-religious people. They believed that only God is perfect. To show their devotion to God, when they made their rugs, they would deliberately include a small faulty stitch, a flaw, into each Persian rug. Similar legends exist in Asia as well as in North and South America. These flaws don't make these rugs less valuable, but more valuable. Though not perfect (without flaw), these rugs are valuable, because they were made with great care and skill. Isn't that what we all want—to live a life with purpose to which we give our very best efforts, even if there is an occasional flaw? Then in the midst of doing the very best we can, our character is strengthened and refined.

ASSEMBLE YOUR LEADERSHIP ADVISORY BOARD

Where do we start when it comes to working with others? We have been taught all our lives to be team players, but rarely have we been told to put together a team. It is interesting and wonderful to know people with talents different than my own. Have you ever said to yourself, *I wish I were more like that person*? Well, we're not and will never be like any other person, because we are all unique. However, our lives can be enriched just the same by the gifts, experience, and advice of others.

How? Assemble your own advisory board to help you be a better leader! Be deliberate. You are forming a leadership advisory board to help you run your most important organization—you! For some this will be a new concept. Regardless, most of you will recognize that you have already put together an impromptu advisory board or team. You may just call them a select group of friends or family members. What I'm suggesting requires you to be more deliberate and exact.

Let's take a look at a typical advisory board member and the legal language that is used in the business world to describe an advisory board member:

- Board members must act honestly and *bona fide* (in good faith).
- A board member shall perform his or her duties in a manner he or she reasonably believes to be in the best interests of the corporation.
- Performs duties with such care as an ordinarily prudent person in a like position with respect to similar corporation would use under similar circumstances.

Can you think of people right away in your circle of family, friends, and acquaintances, from whom you would appreciate getting advice, because they would act "in good faith," have "your best interest," and perform their duty with "care" and "prudence"? You may consider adding board members who would:

- Help with your growth and development
- Listen
- Review your performance and be a trusted accountability adviser
- Give input and advice

- Give support and evaluate your progress
- Validate, affirm, and help you tap into your potential
- Bring expertise that would be helpful to you
- Provide guidance and direction

These people can be living or deceased. They may come from any part of your life. They could be people from throughout history whom you admire. How many board members should you have? How often should you meet, if it's possible? Should the meetings be informal or formal? Do you meet all together or meet with each separately? What should be discussed? You are the chairman of the board. You decide. You may want to add to or change your leadership advisory board as your circumstances change. In the oxen-pull allegory, we mentioned that the winning combination is first, individual strength and training, and secondly, the team's ability and willingness to work together. Working together means your leadership advisory board responds to the same trainer's voice. This is the most important criteria in your selection process. We mentioned the importance of the voice being the voice of strong character. As you consider those you would include in your advisory board, select people with strong character, whose life goals are at least similar to yours. Choose people who use their divine-brains to dominate their thinking. They may have different opinions and abilities, but choose members whose character will strengthen your own. Tap into the power of teams. You have been part of a team of one sort or another at various times throughout your whole life. It is now time to switch your thinking from being a team player to assembling your own team.

On a side note, the impact of putting together a leadership advisory board can be huge at home. Let me give you some insight as to what your parents are more than likely thinking (At least this is what I'm thinking as a parent). Your parents at some point probably worry about what kind of friends you have now and even long before you were a teenager. If you let them know that you are making decisions to:

- Be divinative and make your divine-brain your dominant brain
- Begin and end your day with divine-brain activities
- Continue to move up the Zigzag Path to Growth

- Assemble your advisory board with people who are also divine-brain-dominant

your parents will be thrilled and amazed, and they will sleep better at night. They will know that you are making wise decisions that will not only help you grow now but will also build a solid foundation for a great life.

TEAMWORK DEFINED

Remember that in the oxen-pull contest, the winning combination is individual strength and teamwork. The very best teams consist of two or more people who each have gained great individual strength by the consistent and dominant use of their divine-brains. The members of the team may have different backgrounds, personalities, talents, and skills, but what binds them together is the same commitment to the standards of character and moral strength. This voice is clear, near, and familiar. Teamwork is channeling this trainer's voice of character towards a common goal. The very best teams—whether the teams are families, school teams, work teams, or any other group—are pre-forgiving of themselves and others. Instead of judging and simply confessing the faults of another, they see the faults of others as the monkey-brain and lizard-brain thinking creeping in, and they wisely put all their efforts into helping their teammates get back to divine-brain thinking. They help their family and teammates tune in to the trainer's voice of character, and their teammates help them do the same when needed. The very best teams are full of hope and nurture the divine in others. This is the lesson of the oxen pull. The allegory of the oxen pull is about seeing the value and importance of other people in our lives.

Chapter Quiz:

From the allegory of the oxen pull, to help you become the leader and person you want to be, you need to assemble your

______________ ____________.

It is vitally important that as you select the members of your advisory board, you choose people who use their divine-brain as their dominant brain. True or false?

CHAPTER TEN

ALLEGORY #3: THREE-COMBINATION LOCK

AS you examine your life, even now as a teenager as well as for the rest of your life, you are really trying to lead three lives simultaneously—your life in your community, your family life, and your personal life. Your community life is really a broad definition that includes your school life, life with friends, your extracurricular activities, life as a neighbor, life at church, or any volunteer organization. This is the life where you spend the majority of your time. This is the life where opinions about others and yourself are formed. This is where we make value and character judgments of each other. This is where someone might say we are kind, talented, outgoing, gracious, thoughtful, and so forth.

It's easy to see why we may spend so much time in our community lives and enjoy it. It may be full of friends, acquaintances, and lots of activities with many people. It's nice when people know you, know your name, respect you, and smile when they see you in a crowd of people. This is the life where we feel a sense of belonging. This is where our monkey-brains get really excited. Certainly, having other people singing your praises is very gratifying. Below is a visual representation of time spent mostly in your community life in relation to perhaps your family life and your personal unseen life. If we spend too much time in our community life we may feel disconnected with those in our family life, and our family may feel disconnected with us.

Figure 5: OUR THREE LIVES

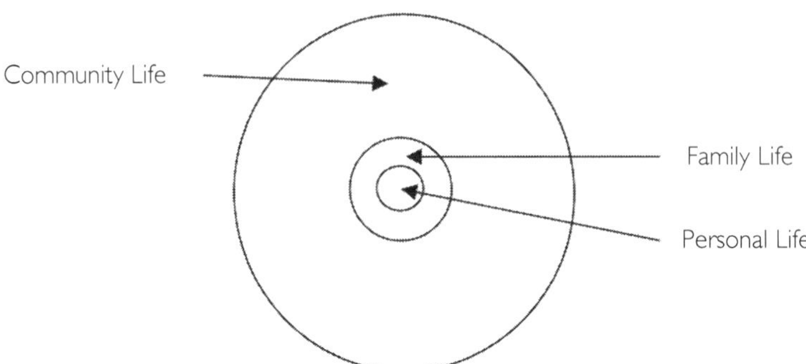

We also have our private lives, which only those few who are closest to us know about. This consists of our family members or a very select group of friends. These are the people we feel most comfortable with, and those with whom we feel we can afford to let our guard down, if you will. These are the people with whom we can share what we really think and feel, and we know they will have the discretion, care, and the wisdom to handle such information. A disconnect between people can occur when each person has a different focus. You may be focused on school and friends. Your parents may be focused on work or all the happenings in the community. Perhaps you have younger siblings and they are in a different world altogether. To keep our relationships strong we need to make sure that we put enough focus on each other and not drift apart.

You may experience a scenario in which a member of your family is consumed with only himself or herself. You may have heard the expression, "I may not be much, but I'm all I think about." Each person at some point, is self-absorbed, trying to answer the question, "Who am I, and where do I fit in?" Figure 6 is a visual representation of three people who focus their time in different areas.

FIGURE 6

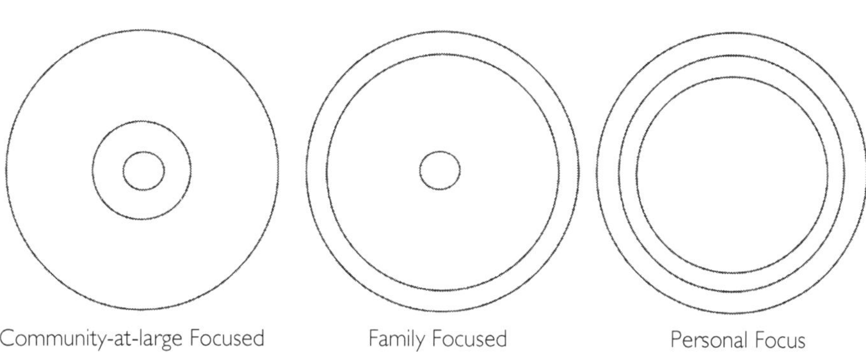

Having members of our family or private lives with a different focus is normal. We are all in different stages with different concerns.

The third life is the unseen personal life. This is the life that only *we, personally* know about. It's sometimes called the secret life. Within our unseen personal lives are our innermost hopes, dreams, struggles, and fears. This is the life where we may feel the strongest and most vulnerable at the same time. This is the life in which we try to reconcile in our hearts, minds, and souls the meaning and value to our existence, in the context of our family and community life as well. This unseen personal life is our core. We know we need to give ample focus to it, while trying to lead busy lives.

These are three interconnected lives indeed, and the importance of each of our three lives will vary, depending on what is going on in that particular season of life. As you look a few years back in your own life, perhaps in your early elementary school years, making time in your personal life, family life, friends, school, sports, music, and everything else was relatively easy. Sure, there were traumatic episodes, crying, new discoveries, deep friendships, big fights, but all of these events seemed to all happen within the same day. Remember how you bounced back quickly, forgave easily, and had short memories? After dinner and a decent night's sleep, you were ready to tackle the big bad world all over again the following day. It seems that the older you get, juggling these three lives become increasingly perplexing and complicated.

As a leader, how do you manage your activities and time in the context of these three lives while those around you are all trying to do the same? Let me suggest three approaches to improvement, from the most common to the most effective.

THREE APPROACHES TO IMPROVEMENT

FIRST: OUTSIDE IN

This is the most common way that each of us hopes change and improvement will occur. The *outside-in* approach basically means that we want everything and everyone to change to suit our needs. It requires the least amount of work and is the least demanding on us personally. Examples could include wishing school and friends were better. Perhaps we would wish our family would see the world as we do and that they would understand us better, without any effort on our part. This is the wishful thinking approach to change. Of course, every once in a while things just work out for us—we may get a teacher at school who is actually pretty cool and the subject is really easy to understand. You may have new friends who just moved into the neighborhood. You might have an unexpected wonderful turn of events. Your parents may not even mention that you should clean your room, do your homework, or get your chores done! This approach has the lowest probability of success and we know it, but we have to try it or at least wish for it, just the same. Ultimately, what we want is an approach that would give us the highest probability of succeeding.

The appeal of the *outside-in* approach is the hope of improvement with the least amount of effort. Juggling your three lives with this outside-in approach is hoping that those in your private or family life and public life or life in the community at large will change or improve on their own, so that you don't have to.

SECOND: INSIDE-OUT

Most people would agree that in the long run an *inside-out* approach is more effective and more predictable than the outside-in approach. The inside-out approach basically means that we need to work on ourselves first. We redefine our challenges from "how circumstances and people should be different (outside-in)" to "how can I be different" (inside-out) to get a different result. When we focus on changing ourselves, we then put less focus on being a victim. We also put greater emphasis where we have the greatest influence—ourselves. When we change, we define the circumstances around us differently. For example, with an outside-in approach we may see the world through the lenses of challenges and problems. Through the inside-out approach, however, we could look at the exact same circumstance and see opportunity and a chance to make a contribution.

> A pessimist sees the difficulty in every opportunity; an optimist sees the opportunity in every difficulty.
>
> —Winston Churchill

A challenge with the inside-out approach, however, is that even though we may mentally agree it is a better approach, sometimes we're not quite sure how to implement it. Based on the Winston Churchill quote about an optimist focusing on the opportunity instead of the difficulty—if we do see things in a pessimistic way, are we supposed to just flip a switch, and all of a sudden we're optimists? We're not quite sure where to begin or what to do next. Another question is, how do we get to the point where we look at the world through an inside-out approach, without feeling like whatever we do is not good enough or that there is always something wrong with us?

THIRD: LIGHT-IN/LEAD-OUT

This third approach is most effective and has elements of the first two approaches. There is a voice within each of us that can sense the answers existing outside ourselves. We know we don't have all the answers, but we also understand that answers do exist out there somewhere, and we need to tap into answers in so many areas of our lives. And so we look for answers outside ourselves—outside-in. We go too far, however, when we expect these answers to come wholly from the outside in, simply for the asking—like a genie in a lamp who can grant to us any three wishes. Of course, we don't limit our outside-in approach to only three wishes. From time to time, we may receive answers in full, but more often, we merely get glimpses and impressions. This is a good thing. Whatever you want to call it, there is a force in the universe that won't give us answers for the asking, but instead gives as hints and gradual insights that we need to diligently work through. If not for this gradual awakening of insights there is the danger of dependence and laziness if we're given the answers too easily. Consider this story from the October 1950 Reader's Digest.

> In our friendly neighbor city of St. Augustine great flocks of sea gulls are starving amid plenty. Fishing is still good, but the gulls don't know how to fish. For generations they have depended on the shrimp fleet to toss them scraps from the nets. Now the fleet has moved ....
>
> The shrimpers had created a Welfare State for the ... sea gulls. The big birds never bothered to learn how to fish for themselves, and they never taught their children to fish. Instead they led their little ones to the shrimp nets.
>
> Now the sea gulls, the fine free birds that almost symbolize liberty itself, are starving to death because they gave in to the "something for nothing" lure! They sacrificed their independence for a handout.

I think people can become like that too. It would be nice if the answers to life's questions were just given to us like scraps or handouts from the universe. However, if life's answers were given to us too easily, it would give us a false sense of security and lull us to laziness that would be just as dangerous to us as it was for these sea gulls in this story. We don't want just the scraps from the universe, anyway. Rather, we want all the universe has to offer. That would require effort on our part. We are trying to prepare ourselves for an unknown and unpredictable future. The Reader's Digest story continues.

> Let's not be gullible gulls. We ... must preserve our talents of self-sufficiency, our genius for creating things for ourselves, our true love of independence.

The fact that effort is required to achieve what we want, is both the challenge and the blessing. Recall the Zigzag Path to Growth in the allegory of the tree. We go through growing pains on our way to personal growth and fulfillment.

LIGHT-IN

This third and most effective way of changing in the "light-in/lead-out" approach has two parts. When we talk about "light-in," think back to the comparison of the lizard-brain, monkey-brain, and divine-brain to the light of the stars, moon, and sun respectively. The brightest of the three heavenly lights is of course the sun. Likewise, the brightest of the three brains is the divine-brain. Light-in means learn from the divine-brain. As you look to make changes and improvements in your life allow the light of the divine-brain illuminate your understanding. Light-in means pay attention and learn from how *other people* who let the light of their divine-brains guide their way through uncertain and unfamiliar paths.

The essence of "light-in" is to understand there are natural laws that govern all results over time. The concept of *law* is great because it implies something that is fixed, predictable, and orderly. These laws, however, are not made by man, nor are they enforced by man. They operate regardless of our awareness, acceptance, or support. They just are. Just as there are laws—such as *gravity*—that govern in the physical dimension, there are natural laws that govern all results. The results may vary in the short term, but in the long-term the results are predictable. It may be helpful to use other words, such as *formulas, principles, rules, recipes, order,* and *blueprints* to clarify the nature of these natural laws. Other synonyms that would help us understand these natural laws are *traits, virtue, character, disposition*, and *quality*. Again they are not just nice trite words. They are the roots that produce the results we want. Just as the Bristlecone Pine and Redwood trees both need nutrients even though their circumstances are vastly different, we need the nutrients that natural laws give us to produce results. Although we'll go into more detail on how to take full advantage of these natural laws in the next chapter, some examples of these natural laws are *vision, empathy, love, pre-forgiveness, contribution,* and *integrity.* These words are not an exhaustive list by any means, and you may choose these and/or other natural laws to govern your life.

The last part of "light-in" is seeing the power and efficacy of these natural laws in the lives of those around us. In short, we need heroes, mentors, and models who live by these natural laws. Heroes, mentors and models are valuable to us because of our three-part brains. Making a conscious decision to live by these natural laws is divine-brain type of thinking. Our monkey-brains, however, are not quite sure what to make of these natural laws—not sure whether it's going to feel good or not so good. When we are not sure whether something will feel good or not, our monkey-brains or that part of us that says social intelligence is important asks, "Who else is doing it, so that we can find out whether they felt good about it or not, and then we'll decide?" Without models, heroes and mentors we hesitate to venture out on our own. Remember, we mentioned how the monkey-brain can hold the divine-brain hostage. Having a model allows our monkey-brains to tell our divine-brains, "It's going to be okay. You'll feel better about it because we discovered that someone else feels good about it, and you respect his and her opinion. Let's go for it."

In the history of mankind, there are those who have gone before us having struggled through similar experiences that we are going through now, though they may not be exactly the same. They have lived their lives based on these natural laws we have mentioned. Without people as examples, words such as *vision* and *integrity* are merely words. They are just abstract ideas. However, when we see these words acted out by those we trust, admire, or rub shoulders with daily, these words become real and powerful to us. Without such examples, we can look at these natural laws and readily dismiss them. We can get so caught up in the uniqueness of our situations that we miss the whole point. We can rationalize ourselves right out of the answers we seek. Our monkey-brains can tell our divine-brains, "I may not know everything, but I don't feel good about this," and then we move on to something else. Light-in is both understanding with the mind and feeling with the heart as we see those we trust live by such natural laws.

Living your life according to natural laws such as vision, empathy, love, contribution, and integrity takes a certain amount of faith, because even though they may produce the results we want over time that may not be the case in the short term. However, expecting high achievement over time without these natural laws doesn't make any sense either. Imagine trying to be the person you want to be and increasing your achievements by being visionless instead of having a clear vision, being cruel instead of empathic, being filled with hatred instead of love, living a life of selfishness instead of contribution, and dealing in corruption instead of integrity. In the long run, having your divine-brain as your dominant brain is better than having your lizard-brain and monkey-brain dominate your life.

When my father was thirty-three years old, he was a high-ranking officer in the Philippine Army. He took great pride in his profession, and he excelled in it. Thinking more about our family than his career, he resigned from the military, and at great expense, we immigrated to the United States. He had to start his career all over again in something else besides the military, not to mention a new country. My parents with their four children lived with our uncle and their family in their small apartment in Los Angeles. I still remember one of his first jobs was at a furniture manufacturing plant. Even as a young boy, I was puzzled as to how he could go from commanding armies—a bright future at the station in life that he had envisioned—to leaving it all behind and taking a lower-paying job that was well below his ability level. Asking him about it as a young man, and still remembering the smile on his face, he said, "Oh that. If my goal had been just for me, we would have stayed. We didn't come here for me. We came here for you." That was my first recollection of really understanding the words *vision, sacrifice, love.* At that moment I wanted to become the kind of man that he is, and I wanted to become the kind of father he is to me. Words such as *vision*, *sacrifice*, and *love* came alive to me as I saw them personified in my mother and father.

Each of you, more than likely, had a person or persons come into your life as a living example of certain character traits. Maybe that person was a parent, grandparent, teacher, neighbor, or friend. Because character is such an integral part of what is means to be a leader, write down the names of three people you admire and who live by the character traits that you want to be known for.

Name ______________________ Character traits lived by _______________
Name ______________________ Character traits lived by _______________
Name ______________________ Character traits lived by _______________

Hopefully you can gain a greater appreciation for those who have been the role models for you. Thank them for the courage they had to live their lives according to natural laws or character traits. Consequently, I hope you can be wiser about the people you select to be part of your leadership advisory board. They can free you and your divine-brain from the bondage that our monkey and lizard-brains can put all of us in. Not only can your advisory board lift you, but they can also give ideas that you have not considered. We all should recognize the impact these role models have on us as well as the impact we have on those who look to us to be their role models.

LEAD-OUT

> Your vision will become clear only when you can look into your own heart. Who looks outside, dreams, who looks inside awakes.
>
> —Carl Jung

Once we learn to allow the light of the divine-brain into our lives, we then have an example, a pattern as to how to lead our lives and how to help others lead their lives—"lead-out." Those who have lived their lives by adhering to natural laws or character traits and have been the type of people we would like to be, serve as examples to us, and their lives become blueprints for us. These wonderful people become our heroes, models, and mentors. Through the lives of these models, we can see, in great detail, their triumphs, the corresponding obstacles, and how to rise above challenges that we wouldn't otherwise anticipate. We pay close attention to what they do, say, think, and even feel. We pay attention to how they prepare to achieve their successes. These people may not be absolutely perfect (without fault), and so we need multiple models. Each of us is unique, so again we need multiple models customized to our unique personalities and circumstances. We look for the very best, the divine, in our heroes and models.

In our private or unseen lives, we begin to live our lives like our models live their lives. We begin to form habits and live our lives according to natural laws and character traits. Like planting a seed, in time, our habits of *vision, empathy, love, contribution*, and *integrity* blossom and bear fruit. Not only do they bear fruit, but they do so time and time again. The more we see desirable results, the more our confidence grows in our hearts as well as in our minds. These habits that we form are not just stuff we put on a list and check off as we do them, but rather, these natural laws change our very nature.

Once we can sense that our very nature is changing, it is so exciting. We get so invigorated by the positive results from living according to strong character traits that we want to share it with those in our family and others in our private lives. As our own lives transform and improve we are compelled to want to help our loved ones transform and improve as well. We, in turn, become models for others. If our lives have truly been lifted, we want to lift the lives of others.

Light-in and lead-out takes effort, but it is well worth the effort. I hope your results and your excitement make you not only want to share with your families, but that you would also want to share with those in your community life—your neighborhoods, friends, and even strangers, for that matter. Share your experience and insight as to how deliberately improving your character has helped you.

This approach of light-in then lead-out makes sense to people, because we have all experienced it to some degree. Look at it this way. Think again of the person who saw you better than you saw yourself? Because such a person has come along, he or she has lighted your way (light-in). Because someone has become the source of light or inspiration for you, haven't you in turn wanted to become the source of light and inspiration for someone else (lead-out)?

> What man actually needs is not a tensionless state, but rather the striving and struggling for some goal worthy of him. What he needs is not the discharge of tension at any cost, but the call of a potential meaning waiting to be fulfilled by him.
>
> —Victor Frankl

Ultimately, what teenagers want is to have a rich personal life, rich family life, and wonderful relationships and friendships. In the context of our three lives, we want to unlock and unleash the potential we all feel is inside of us. Look at it as a three-combination lock that you probably use in school. Do you remember the directions to open your combination lock? You had to turn the dial clockwise to a specific number lined up to a notch and then turn to the left for the second number until you passed the second number for the second time around. You then turned clockwise again to the third number, and when you pulled on the shackle, the lock would open. What would happen to me, however, was that every now and then, in my rush, I would only turn counterclockwise to the second number once instead of twice, before turning clockwise to the third number. When I pulled the shackle, it wouldn't open. There was no other way to get the combination lock to work other than to start over and try again. There were no shortcuts on the combination lock. It is much the same way with our three interconnected lives. If we want to unlock and unleash the full potential that is in each of us like the unlocking of a combination lock, there is a process that works—and there are no shortcuts. Light-in then lead-out.

The lesson from the allegory of the Bristlecone Pine and Redwood trees is how to continuously grow while at the same time fight our fires from without and avoid disease from within. Although there is much we can do individually to grow, the allegory of the oxen pull reminds us how we also need others as we pull our life's load. The lesson of the allegory of the three-combination lock is to have the context of the three lives we lead and the need to learn how others have led their lives by the light of their divine-brain (light-in)—and after we learn from others we need to live the same way and be examples for others around us (lead-out). We need to take a look at the next allegory of the four seasons to take a deeper look at how exactly we implement "light-in." What follows the allegory of the four seasons—the allegory of the five golden rings—will allow us to take a deeper look at how exactly we "lead-out."

Chapter Quiz:

We all try to juggle three lives:

Our ____________ life
Our ____________ life
Our_____________ life

What are the three approaches to change?

When looking at change from the "Light-In/Lead-Out" approach, what does this mean to you?

CHAPTER ELEVEN

ALLEGORY #4: FOUR SEASONS

IMAGINE the four seasons: winter, spring, summer, and autumn. They happen in a predictable sequence, and each season plays an important part in the ecosystem. Plants, animals, and people alike respond to the rhythm of the seasons. Each season gives its distinctive beauty and feeling as well as bringing balance to the ecology.

This allegory is connected to how we achieve desirable results consistently. Achieving desirable results also has seasons, sequences, and patterns. As we have just examined in the allegory of the three-combination lock, we mentioned the definition and importance of light-in and lead-out. In this allegory we are going to take a more in-depth look at light-in. We will not only look at how results are achieved, but how character is connected to results.

One of the four seasons represents our achievements. How do we realize achievements, and what is the predictable pattern to achieving them? Consider this question. Would you agree with me if I said that your achievements stem from the things that you do and/or say? In the many times I have posed this question the answer has always been *yes*. It is obvious and self-evident. What we do and say has a great impact on what we achieve. Desirable results or achievements represent one season. The things we do and say that lead to our achievements represents a second season.

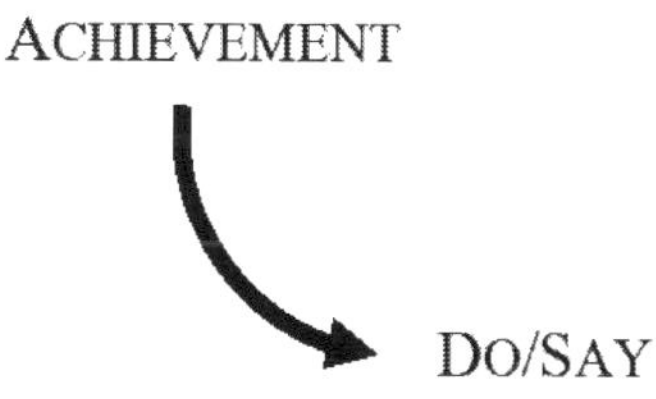

To illustrate, consider for example, an athlete who practices his sport for hours each day. When the practices (do/say) have been done repeatedly and done well, the athlete or team is likely to do well during competition (achievements). Think about a teenager who spends quality time with parents or siblings playing, listening, working together, laughing (do/say), and consequently have good relationships (achievements). It's easy to see how consistency in actions and in words contributes to your achievements.

> If people knew how hard I worked to get my mastery, it wouldn't seem so wonderful at all.
>
> —Michelangelo

In the last chapter you wrote down the names of three people you admire and who live according to the character traits you want to emulate in your own life. To further examine and validate the notion that achievements come from what you do and say, think about these admirable people and ask the following questions.

- What extraordinary results did they achieve?
- What particular actions did they take that led directly to their remarkable achievements?
- What were they consistently doing and/or saying that helped produce better results time and time again, where others who may have the same ability weren't as productive?

The deeper you dig into the success you see in others, the more you will realize that, like Michelangelo, there is a predictable pattern of effort and hard work that leads to achieving results. The more you peer into the lives of those you admire, the more you will realize that in many respects, they are just normal people like you and me, complete with weaknesses as well as strengths. They did and continue to do what most of us have the potential to do, but these role models were just more deliberate and consistent.

Watching ordinary people do extraordinary things by being consistent in what they do and say is such a hopeful thought. If they can do it, you can as well. The question is figuring out how these wonderful people are so consistent where others stall. We'll get to that.

Again, one of the seasons in this allegory represents our achievements. A second season is what we do and or say. Yet another season is what we think and feel. Would you also agree with me if I said that what we do and say is influenced by what we are thinking and feeling at that given moment? Like the previous question, when I ask this of different groups of people, time and time again, the answer is a resounding *yes.* It would be the same for us, our role models, or anyone, for that matter. It would also be the same regardless of whether we were looking at great achievements or bad results.

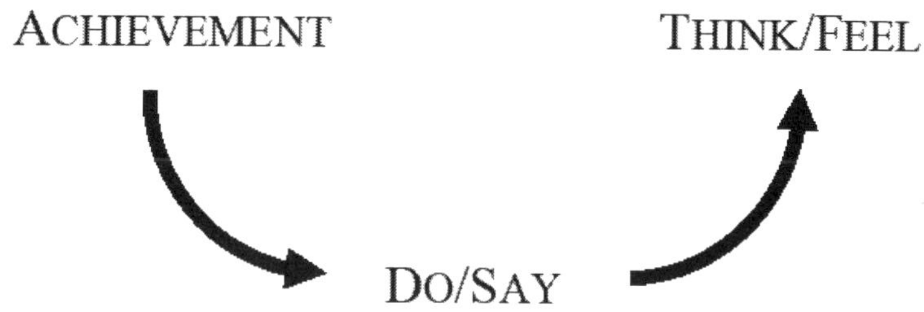

Many people striving to achieve different results have an unrelenting focus on taking different actions. This makes sense, but it's incomplete. You have probably heard the expression that the definition of insanity is doing the same things and expecting different results. It's natural to think that doing things differently would produce different results. This makes sense when we make our grand plans but they seldom last. As with most New Year's resolutions, we're doing great on January 1st, but we usually don't make it to February 1st.

Here's something else to think about. Have you ever had friends ask for your advice and they want to know what you think they should *do?* Have you noticed that sometimes, after you give them your wise advice, they then proceed to tell why your advice simply won't work? Why does that happen? It happens because we may come to an agreement on what to *do,* but we are not in agreement on how we *think* or *feel* about taking those actions. For example, we may all agree that exercise and eating a healthy diet is a good thing to *do*, but when it comes time to actually *do* what we know we should, we can *think* of reasons why not to exercise or eat right on a given day, or we just may not *feel* like doing them today.

> He who cannot change the very fabric of his thought will never be able to change reality, and will never, therefore, make any progress.
>
> —Anwar el-Sadat

Once again think back to your role models whom you admire, and evaluate how they were able to think/feel differently than most, and how it allowed them to take different actions that most wouldn't take. Ask them how they were able to make the shift in their thinking and feeling. This is a great exercise, because it will give you great insight on what motivates you and what motivates others.

Let me give you another example of the power of how we think and feel. I have seen students get bad grades in high school, yet when they got to college, they did extremely well. Normally students do well in high school, and as classes are tougher in college they don't fare as well. It seems backwards at first. However, looking more closely at these students who do better in college than in high school, I discovered that these students were bright and more than capable. Unfortunately they saw no purpose in their education while in high school. When they got to college the light bulb turned on in their hearts and minds, and they really applied themselves and their grades went up significantly.

Again, results and achievements come from what we do/say. What we want to *do* and *say* can only be sustained when they are in alignment with what we *really think* and *really feel*. In the simple examples on exercise and eating right, the model is obvious. In the more important issues in our lives the model works just as well, but it requires a bit more soul searching. For example, what do you *really* think and feel about yourself? What do you *really* think about the important people in your life? Are some of those important relationships strained? How do you really feel about those people? What do you *really* think and feel about your outlook on the future and the unique contributions you can make? In your quiet and private moments you need to reconcile what you sincerely think and feel. No one except for you can answer this do/say think/feel alignment question in the tough issues for you. This takes humility and honesty and some time to ponder. Remember the distance between heaven and hell. When you reconcile your real intent, your true feelings, and most honest opinions, it is a great victory indeed. Going through this exercise of accurately assessing your thoughts and feelings will give you clarity.

Let's have a quick review. The results and achievements we get stem from the things we do and/or say. What we do and say is influenced by what we think and feel. This begs the question, "If what we do and say is influenced by what we think and feel, what then molds what we think and feel?" In short, it's the voice that we listen to. Remember the allegory of the oxen pull and the trainer's voice? Ultimately then, the voice that we listen to directly impacts our achievements.

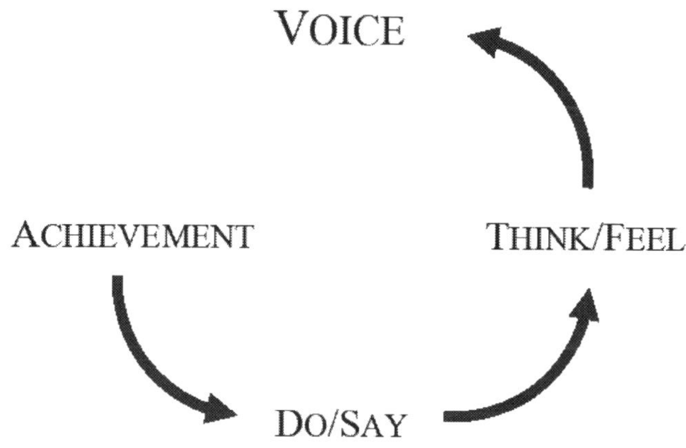

Now let's take a closer look at the voice you may listen to that affects your thoughts and feelings. There are many external voices that demand your attention. There are the voices from society as a whole, the media, television, radio, movies, music, computer games, neighbors, school, friends, family, and other relationships. Each of these voices has an impact on you, however large or small. Some of these voices stimulate your lizard-brain and monkey-brain, while others are just noise without much value. Just to give you a reality check on the impact of these external voices, list your top five television shows, movies, songs, video games, and figure out whether they predominantly give you lizard-brain, monkey-brain, or divine-brain messages.

Again, lizard-brain messages are mostly survival messages. The themes are "eat or be eaten," competition, comparison, winner take all, win or go home, and the like. Monkey-brain messages are doing whatever it takes to fit it and feel included or doing what feels good at the moment and worry about the consequences later. Divinative messages are higher-order thinking such as contribution, love, service, compassion, integrity, wisdom, and so forth. As you examine these voices some are strictly lizard-brain, monkey-brain, or divine-brain. Other voices have a mix but one still dominates. Fox example, by definition a sporting event is predominantly lizard-brain. It's about competition and survival. However the television network may also briefly include a heartwarming story about one of the athletes, but the dominant message and voice of the show still goes back to competition. So come up with your favorite television shows, movies, songs, and video games and label them "L" for lizard-brain dominant, "M" for monkey-brain dominant, or "D" for divine-brain dominant.

My favorite television shows are:	L, M, D
______________________________	__________
______________________________	__________
______________________________	__________
______________________________	__________
______________________________	__________

My favorite movies are:	L, M, D
______________________________	__________
______________________________	__________
______________________________	__________
______________________________	__________
______________________________	__________

My favorite songs are:	L, M, D
______________________________	__________
______________________________	__________
______________________________	__________
______________________________	__________
______________________________	__________

My favorite video games are:	L, M, D
______________________________	__________
______________________________	__________
______________________________	__________
______________________________	__________
______________________________	__________

Did you have any surprises as you went through that exercise? Asking groups from different parts of the world to go through this exercise, most are surprised at how many lizard-brain and monkey-brain voices they experience on a daily basis and how few divine-brain messages even exist. Can you see why having divine-brain activities first thing in the morning and last thing at night is so important? It gives you a break from the lizard-brain and monkey-brain messages you hear all day long. Can you appreciate why the Zigzag Path to Growth can help you rise above lizard-brain and monkey-brain messages and help you be a better leader, awakening your awesomeness within?

Now that you have taken inventory of how many lizard-brain, monkey-brain, and divine-brain voices surround you each day, what's next? All day long, every day, we receive lizard-brain, monkey-brain and divine-brain messages and voices in different degrees. Yet not every person responds to them the same way. Why? Remember, in the very beginning of the book we said that leadership is lifting others to the standards you are inspired to earnestly live. Where do these standards come from? They come from sifting through all of the lizard-brain, monkey-brain, and divine-brain voices and messages and filtering them through our internal voice.

We'll go through it in greater depth in the fifth allegory, but imagine you are trying to find gold. When mining gold you use a lot of filters. You first collect a lot of earth where you suspect there is gold. You then get rid of boulders, rocks, gravel, and dirt using filters until you get to the gold. I'm over simplifying it, but you get the idea. Similarly every person gets a lot of lizard-brain, monkey-brain and divine-brain messages all day long, every day. You use your internal voice of character to filter out the voices you don't want and get to the voice or the standards you are inspired to live. After a while, you get really quick with differentiating between lizard-brain, monkey-brain, and divine-brain voices. You get rid of what you don't want and keep what you do want. At first you may be unsure and so you take it all in, but in time you become more selective.

Another example and parallel might be shopping for clothes. If you're not sure what you want, when you shop for clothes you go to every store trying on every piece of clothing imaginable. As you get more shopping experience, after a while not only do you not try everything on, you even narrow down the stores where you will shop. When you do shop in the stores you prefer, you know what styles you want and which styles you are sure you do not want to be seen wearing in public. From the styles that are acceptable, you will try on a few and decide which one is worth your money to buy. Choosing the standards you are inspired to earnestly live requires you to do some shopping, if you will, using your internal voice of character and making a choice. Listen to and be true to your inner voice of character. Your own inner voice of character should be the voice that lets you know what value and attention you should give to all the external voices.

> The only tyrant I accept in this world is the still voice within.
>
> —Mahatma Gandhi

In my profession, I work with a lot of teachers throughout the United States and Canada. When asking teachers about students who struggle in school, whether it's about grades or getting in trouble, I ask them what they think the biggest contributor to the students' challenges is. Without exception, educators observe that those who struggle are the students who listen too much to the external voices that are lizard-brain and monkey-brain focused in their neighborhoods—television, music, movies, peer pressure, video games—and not enough to the voices that are divine-brain focused that shape their own inner voices of character. I get the same answer if I ask elementary school teachers, middle school teachers, high school teachers, or even college professors. It can get tougher the older you get, because you have access to more lizard-brain and monkey-brain voices. It can also get easier the older you get if you can learn to use the filter of you internal voice well.

You need to be selective as to which voices to listen to. Part of what you need to do as a leader is to figure out how you will reduce or eliminate the time you spend listening to voices that do not lead you towards your best self. Do not spend time with people or situations that are at odds with your divine voice. Spend more time with people and in places that are uplifting and can validate your awesomeness, your divine voice, your character.

Make divine-brain choices every day in small, consistent ways, and you'll find that making divine-brain choices in big ways will be easier. To illustrate the importance of making small, deliberate decisions, think about your favorite picture. Every picture is collection of pixels. When you are close enough to the picture to examine each particular pixel, none of these pixels is particularly impressive or interesting. Stand a little further back, and you will see a combination of pixels with different colors—probably going in different directions—and they may seem completely random. It is not until you stand back far enough to see the entire picture and get the appropriate context that you will see a beautiful picture. Similarly, when we evaluate the character of those we admire, we will see that they do good things consistently, or that they develop their character deliberately, one pixel at a time. Like looking at a picture too closely, small and deliberate acts to improve character may not seem like much. Collectively, these seemingly small acts, as you persist, can make of your life a work of art.

No man can climb out beyond the limitations of his own character.

—John Morley

No matter how full a reservoir of maxims one may possess, and no matter how good one's sentiments may be, if one has not taken advantage of every concrete opportunity to act, one's character may remain entirely unaffected for the better.

—William James

ACHIEVEMENT CYCLE

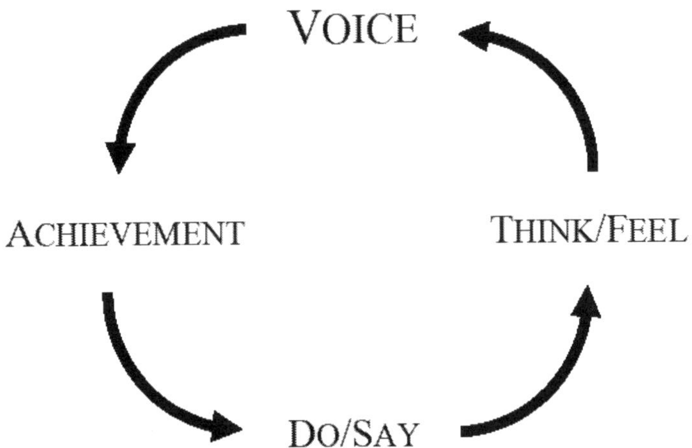

I refer to this cycle as the Achievement Cycle. Initially we looked at this model in a counter-clockwise direction to explain the way it works. Go through your own counter-clockwise examination of your life and get a good sense of your current reality. Start with achievements and go counter-clockwise from there. Then go clockwise beginning with voice and follow the cycle, making the appropriate additions, deletions, and modifications to be the leader and person you want to be.

As you look at the four seasons and the Achievement Cycle, making changes begins with listening to the divine voice of character, which to me, is synonymous with the winter season. Winter is a period of reflection and a new beginning. The winter solstice marks the victory of light over darkness. Winter begins the new cycle of light, life, and growth, and so it is with listening to the voice of character and figuring out the standards you want to live by. A focus on the development of your character represents a victory and greater dominance of your divine-brain over your lizard-brain and monkey-brain. Listening to the voice of character and committing yourself to a set of standards enlightens our hearts and minds. It marks a new beginning of growth in the Achievement Cycle. Listening to the voice of character and self-chosen standards gives greater life to our divine-brains.

As spring follows winter, so do our thoughts and feelings spring from our character and standards. Spring represents a time of blossoming. Spring is a time when the weather becomes more temperate. Spring is a period of optimism, of a rebirth, and renewal. Similarly, as you are going in the clockwise direction in the Achievement Cycle and focusing on listening to your inner voice of character and standards, your thoughts and feelings will blossom and become more refined, hopeful, and peaceful. Your thoughts will become more temperate. There will still be ups and downs, but you will discover that emotionally you will become more even and more temperate. Your view of life will be more optimistic as you see the best in yourself and others. You will have a rebirth and a renewal in your faith in all people. Of course, not everything will change immediately, but you will see more of the potential and awesomeness in yourself and others.

Next comes the summer. The summer days are also the longest days of the year in which daylight predominates. Summer days are the warmest days of the year. With the longest days come the shortest nights. Summers are filled with activity and celebration. Summer is a time of festivals, holidays, gatherings, and vacations. Summers give the feeling that time is suspended, and everything seems possible. The parallel for summer in the Achievement Cycle is what we do and say. When your actions and words are deliberate expressions of your character and personal standards, then your actions and words are filled with that divine light that is within you. Like the summer season, your divine light dominates, and you act with faith and confidence. When you actions flow from your character and personal standards, everything seems possible, and your actions are inspired and seem effortless.

The last of our four seasons is autumn. Autumn is the season of harvest. As you progress clockwise in the Achievement Cycle, you will harvest greater achievements, and your inner voice of character and personal standards will seem even more familiar, nearer, and clearer. With each successive cycle, your confidence in yourself, your character and standards, and this model will grow. With each cycle you will awaken the awesomeness and divine within you.

Let's do a quick review in our leadership journey from the allegory of the combination lock, to the allegory of the four seasons.

- In the spirit of light-in then lead-out, make a list of people you admire.
- From among the people you admire, choose role models who exemplify the character traits you would want to emulate in your own life.
- Go through the Achievement Cycle and learn how your chosen role models and mentors realized their awesomeness.
- Examine their lives by looking at the voice of character and standards they chose to live by, followed by how your role models think and feel differently as a result of using these character traits as their moral codes.
- Examine the behaviors that come from their thoughts and feelings. Also look at the words they say. How are their words and actions different, compared to those who achieved less?
- Look at the results they have achieved as a result of their behaviors and words.

Go through this process a number of times with different people. Choose people you know personally, and even take a look at great people in history and see whether the model of the Achievement Cycle holds up. Ask your role models and mentors about their role models and mentors, and find out if the Achievement Cycle fits for those people as well. Go through the Achievement Cycle a number of times, clockwise and counterclockwise.

If you want to diagnose how results, good or bad, came to fruition, begin by identifying the results. Let's start with good results. Begin by examining one of the proudest accomplishments of your life. Write it down in the line below.

Proud Accomplishment: ______________________________

Beginning with your result or accomplishment, go counterclockwise in the Achievement Cycle and identify the actions you took and the words you spoke that directly led to your amazing accomplishment. Now we want to isolate your particular behaviors and words. Continuing in the counter-clockwise direction, identify thoughts and feelings that motivated you to act and speak as you did. Finally, pinpoint the character trait(s) and personal standards you had to draw from as well as the deep desires that you had in your heart of hearts to accomplish what you did. Please take the time and opportunity to celebrate not just your achievements but your strength of character and personal standards necessary to achieve your remarkable results. Can you see how all the components of the Achievement Cycle contribute to and explain your accomplishment?

It's important to go through the same examination regarding negative results as well as regarding the very best results. Seeing the contrast will help you recognize where your breakdowns occur and give you clues as to how to correct them. The more familiar you are with the model, the quicker you can anticipate where the corrections are most needed in your life. If examining your bad results feels too painful or you think those experiences are too close for you to objectively examine them, turn on the news on TV or the Internet. There's usually a story about someone who has been very successful and has recently fallen from grace, causing us to view that person much differently than we did before. Go through the Achievement Cycle to see if you can match the rise and fall of these people with this model. You may get new insights. Whether you examine good results or bad, this Achievement Cycle will usually go back to the strength of character and personal standards or lack thereof. I say *usually,* because like the weather, we can have natural disasters in our lives that cannot be foreseen, or we may have wonderful weather that we didn't anticipate. So, you may see an exception here or there. In the long run, however, our results will follow this model.

Now that you have gone through this cycle by looking at your successes in the past, ask yourself what else you want to accomplish in the future. You are a teenager and your whole life is ahead of you. Once you understand the Achievement Cycle, you can see more clearly how you can diagnose your past successes as well as failures through the same model. You can put this model to use in carrying out your future triumphs.

Chapter Quiz:

Draw lines matching the four seasons with the different parts of the Achievement Cycle.

Summer	Think/Feel
Spring	Do/Say
Autumn/Fall	Voice/Standards
Winter	Achievements

What are the three types of external voices we can listen to?

As we use our internal voice of character to filter external voices, what remains are our ________________.

CHAPTER TWELVE

ALLEGORY #5: FIVE GOLDEN RINGS

FROM the lesson of the allegory of the three-combination lock, we know we are trying to balance three lives:

1) Our personal or unseen lives
2) Our private or family lives
2) Our public lives or our lives in the community at large

To unlock and unleash our awesomeness within, the most effective way to improve and change is to allow light-in, meaning learning from other people's triumphs and successes. After light-in we lead-out by understanding and following the Achievement Cycle. Light-in is the lesson taught in the allegory of the four seasons. We diagnose our lives or someone else's life, by moving counterclockwise in the Achievement Cycle, using achievements as our starting point. We then make the appropriate changes in our lives by moving clockwise in the Achievement Cycle. The most critical piece of the Achievement Cycle is paying attention to the external voices we listen to. Take these external voices and then with the use of our internal voice of character as our filter, come up with and commit to the standards we want to live our lives. From these standards or our self-chosen voice will flow what we think and feel, which impacts what we do and say, which will then lead to our achievements.

So now that we have covered what it means to allow the light-in, the next step is to take what we have learned from others and lead-out. The question this brings up, however, is how to make sure we have a large enough reservoir of character strength when we need it, instead of falling back to lizard-brain or monkey-brain thinking. In other words, how do we make sure the standards we want to live by to be a leader is strong enough?

The development of our character and the standards we are inspired to live parallels the process of finding, producing, and ultimately making use of gold. The allegory of the five golden rings refers to the five processes needed to make use of gold. Developing our self-chosen standards or character is also a five-part process. The first three revolve around developing ourselves. The last two parts of developing the voice, character, and standards we want to live by involve applying what we have learned in our homes and the community-at-large. The parallel steps are:

- Prospecting
- Mining
- Extracting
- Refining
- Use

Prospecting

Gold is present in almost all rocks and soil, but in most instances it is in such small quantities that it is invisible to the naked eye. Only in those areas where the concentration is large enough, is it profitable to mine gold. Scientists, sometimes referred to as prospectors, look for areas where there are higher concentrations of gold—enough to take the next step—mining.

Similarly, when we consider character traits and personal standards we wish to develop, all of them exist within each of us, to varying degrees. With each individual, like the gold in soils and rock, metaphorically speaking, different character traits and personal standards are in great abundance, while other character traits are invisible to the naked eye. You may recognize that *compassion*, for example, exists in great abundance and concentration within one person, and exists in less visible quantities within another person. Regardless, compassion is there. Certainly, all character traits are worth mining, so to speak, but we want to work on those traits that we have in the greatest abundance and purity.

Let's go back to the prospecting of gold. Sometimes when prospectors find deposits of gold, it is indeed pure gold. In most of the gold deposits, however, gold is combined with other metals such as silver. It requires further investigation to determine the amount of gold that exists in the area. When these gold deposits are found, scientists will drill down below the surface, gather samples, and analyze further to decide whether the amount of gold present is worth the effort to mine.

Much as gold can in found in purity in some cases, but combined with other metals most of the time, so are our character traits. They are intermingled. For example, the character trait of charity more likely is connected with the character traits of service and empathy. This is a wonderful thing, because as we give focus on developing one character trait, we can't help but develop other character traits as well.

Our initial effort is in figuring out which character trait to work on first. Choosing character traits to focus on first isn't intended to limit us, but it's simply intended to select our strongest character traits to build a foundation. Ask yourself which character traits are worth your time and effort to mine, refine, and ultimately use first. There are a couple of tests we can do, much as the prospectors drill down and analyze, to choose their priorities. The first suggestion is to think of character traits in people whom you admire and would want to emulate in your own life. There are certain qualities we admire in others, because with some, we see those same traits already in ourselves. We just want to magnify them or bring them closer to our lives. Just as prospectors sometimes need to look below the surface of the earth to find high concentrations of gold, so we need to look more deeply and introspectively. However, we already know (don't we) in our heart of hearts, what we can be (as it relates to character) even if others don't know. There are some character traits you may have carefully hidden from others. Those hidden traits need to come out to bless your life and contribute to those around you.

Another suggestion would be to ask the help of your advisory board that was mentioned in the allegory of the oxen pull. Asking for advice from your advisory board is analogous to scientists gathering samples to analyze the concentration of gold. Your advisory board members have enough samples of your strongest character traits that they have gathered about you over the years. Ask them. You may not choose to ask all of them, but there are those with whom you can comfortably have a frank conversation about your character traits. You will find that as you ask multiple members of your advisory board, you will hear patterns and recurring themes that will let you know where your greatest strengths lie and what your strongest character traits are. You may have a tendency to be shy about your character traits, and especially if one of them is *humility.* Identifying your character traits is not about being prideful, but it's about identifying the strongest divine light (light-in) that is in you sufficiently so that you can then prepare to lead-out. In that spirit, after you have drilled down and done your analysis, what are those character traits that you would want to refine to pure gold?

Write a few of them down.

____

____

____

You cannot get this exercise wrong, because as gold is sometimes mixed with other precious metals such as silver, so is one character trait connected to another. Also, remember that this is just one pass at this, but you can go through this exercise as many times as you want. As you identify the character traits that are in abundance within you, celebrate them. Seriously! You are a person of great worth who has much to contribute to others. You have been blessed and given these character traits as your special gifts, and they can become a blessing to others, much the same as the character traits you admire in others have strengthened and continue to strengthen you. As you celebrate your strengths, make a "note to self." *Continue being* _______ (insert character traits). The celebration of your character traits is not just a good idea but a critical step in this process—and the celebration can't be skipped. The more you look at your strengths, the more grateful you will be for your uniqueness. Ask yourself the following questions:

- What are my strongest character traits? (Select at least three)
- In what ways have I lived them in my live so far?
- How have my character traits been a blessing to others?
- How do I feel when I act according to these character traits?

- What motivates me to act according to these character traits?

The reason for looking at yourself this way is not just to get an appreciation for you strengths and character, but to have a personal experience with your heart and mind (remember the distance between heaven and hell section of this book), what it feels like to have your character traits appreciated. Remember the third allegory of the three-combination lock? Light-in then lead-out. As we lead-out, only after we go through the process of appreciating and truly celebrating our strengths and genuinely knowing from experience what that feels like, can we help our loved ones and then others see the character traits within themselves. You need to know how to receive before you can know how to give. You will discover how to help others mine their golden character traits and celebrate their strengths once you have recognized your own. This is the essence of the first part of building your character and the standards you want to live by. Identify your character traits or standards you want to live by, celebrate them, and continue living according to them.

The development of our character starts by being and doing what we already know we should be and do consistently. You may be asking yourself "If magnifying character traits ultimately leads to achievements, are there some character traits that are *better* than others?" It's not the character traits that matter as much as how we deliberately and consistently apply them that make the difference. The other thing to consider is that your unique combination of character traits may be easier for you to live by and harder for someone else, and vice versa. This is about making the most of *your* character traits and not someone else's.

Mining

Let's go back again to the process of refining gold. Once the prospector has determined there is sufficient gold, he will set up a mining operation. Mining usually involves the use of explosives. Sometimes gold is found close to the surface of the earth, and then open-mine techniques are used. Other times the gold is deeper inside the earth, and underground-mining processes are used. Either way, explosives are used to break up the ground. In parts of the world where explosives are not used or are not available, a great deal of manual labor is required instead. There's no going around the mining process. For gold to be of any use, it must be separated from the earth. From the mines, the rocks and soil are then loaded in trucks and hauled to the mill.

The second step in the development of your character requires separation, just like the gold needing to be separated from the earth to be refined. The process of character development and leadership development may take a completely different approach. It may require blowing up how you thought about leadership in the past. It may require a great deal of labor and a coordinated effort from a number of people. It will more than likely require all of the above.

If we are going to develop our character so we can lead, our lives cannot remain as they are, unexamined and unchanged. Remember that the reason for examining and strengthening our character stems from the understanding that the results and achievements we get in life are a function of how our character meets the challenges we face. I put it in an equation below. It may seem a little weird, but share and explain it to an adult, and it will impress him or her.

$$\text{ACHIEVEMENTS} = \text{FUNCTION of} \left(\frac{\text{VOICE OF CHARACTER}}{\text{DIFFICULTY OF THE CHALLENGE}} \right)$$

The more difficult the challenge, the greater and stronger the character required. The greater the achievement we want, again the greater the character needed. This separation we are referring to requires leaving behind what is not needed and taking up what is absolutely necessary. Another word closely related to *separation* in the context of building character is *sacrifice.* The root of the word sacrifice is *sacred.* Sacrifice requires letting go. My intent in mentioning separation and sacrifice is to identify the next step to the development of our character, and it is a very common process for all of us. Anytime we sacrifice or let something go, what remains is more sacred. It is more sacred because we have paid a price for it. Even something as simple as giving a kind word, a good deed, or writing a "thank-you" note, requires sacrificing our time, effort, thought, and attention. What will remain—the words, the memory of good deeds, and the relationship—are more sacred. Think back to when you helped someone who was sick, and you gave of yourself, your time, and your love. After your service and sacrifice, you were changed, and your soul felt better.

Consider your own experience when you excelled and grew as a person. When you participated in sports or band or any other extracurricular activities in school, for example, didn't you make sacrifices? Instead of taking an afternoon nap or hanging out with friends after school, you were separated from the comforts of your bed or from hanging out with friends and you attended practice. In addition to practice after school, you probably put in additional hours to improve on your own, which may have required some practice on the weekends. This meant even more separation and sacrifice. When the price you paid in practice translates to a win in a sporting event or a great performance, the accomplishment is more meaningful or sacred.

The second step in the development of our character and leadership requires sacrifice. Developing the character trait of *love*, for example, may require the sacrifice of letting go of prejudices and truly listening and understanding the other person. It may require forgiveness. We'll need to let go of our lizard-brain and monkey-brain thoughts of vengeance and let go of the pain from being offended.

> To err is human, to forgive divine.
>
> —Alexander Pope

Developing the character trait of love may require pre-forgiveness and always seeing the divine in ourselves and others. Sacrificing lizard-brain and monkey-brain thinking may be required. Mining the character trait of love may require the sacrifice of greater thoughtful service. It may require getting out of our comfort zones. In any case, the mining of character requires sacrificing whatever is needed to give us the opportunity to refine our character. The opposite is to get lazy and try to find the most efficient way out. This would be a mistake. This isn't about speed but character and leadership building. Take the time to give of yourself generously. Selfishness is something else that may need to be sacrificed or separated from our hearts and minds.

Each of these five steps builds on each other. Just as prospecting has to happen first before mining can occur, identifying your strongest character traits has to happen first before sacrificing to make your character traits even stronger and more sacred can occur. After identifying a character trait that you want to magnify, the next natural step in character and leadership development is to go above and beyond what you are already doing through sacrifice.

I can't imagine a more worthwhile goal than the development of your character. It prepares you to get the results and achievement you want. It does, however, take time and focus. Give character development a high enough priority and take the time to work on it. Reaching excellence in anything you do requires sacrifice and separation, and it is no different in reaching for excellence in your character.

Extracting

The third step in the gold-refining process is called extracting. Remember, the first step is prospecting or finding where the gold concentration is high enough to go to the next step—mining. Mining is separating the gold from the earth and taking it to the mill. Extracting is what happens in the mill. It is a complex process. First the rocks are crushed to the size of gravel and then crushed again to powder. The powder then goes through a series of screens, and chemical solvents are used in the extracting process, so what remains is mostly gold.

The third step in the character development process is learning. Just as gold goes through a myriad of steps to separate everything from the gold, character development goes through a purifying process involving activities such as studying, pondering, reflecting, meditating, reading, and even journal writing. As you go through these activities, you will learn and unlearn what is necessary to build your character. This is a very private and personal exercise, and each person will learn and unlearn in his or her own unique way. What is common in the end, however, is making a commitment to live according to our strongest character traits. The allegory of the tree included the need for prayer and meditation as well as studying the scriptures and other inspirational literature. The intent there was to assist in helping your divine-brain become the dominant brain. The learning that we are speaking of here is a continuation of that development.

> None of us will ever accomplish anything excellent or commanding except when he listens to this whisper which is heard by him alone.
>
> —Ralph Waldo Emerson

Learning Process

As I have observed those who make a serious commitment to learning any field of study or topic, especially learning to build their character, they go through a similar learning process. I wish I would have known what I'm about to share when I was going to school. Studying would have been a lot more fun and it would have made more sense. Henry Bloom studied our objectives as we learn new things. He organized these objectives form the lowest level (1) to the highest (6). Another word for organizing or classifying these objectives is *taxonomy*. So the following are referred to as Bloom's taxonomy.

6) Creating
5) Evaluating
4) Analyzing
3) Applying
2) Understanding
1) Remembering

Notice how they all end in "ing." They are all verbs. They all ask us to act. The interesting thing is many of the tests you take in school focus mostly on remembering and understanding, or the bottom two levels. Tests are less likely to involve analyzing, evaluating, and creating—the highest levels of learning. It's also interesting that the highest-paid jobs require the most analyzing, evaluating, and creating. So when you study, don't be satisfied with just remembering and understanding your school work, but push yourself to analyze, evaluate, and create. By the way, all of your teachers know Bloom's taxonomy, so if you want to impress them, ask them to explain Bloom's taxonomy to you and ask them how they are using it to teach you. You will find that your very best teachers purposefully help you to get to the highest levels. Ask them to help you get to the highest levels.

So how do you apply Bloom's taxonomy to character development? Let me give you an example to illustrate. Let's say you want to know about *integrity*. From studying the word, you know that integrity means to adhere to moral and ethical principles. The root of the word integrity is integer (In math an integer is a whole number.). To have integrity means to be whole.

Hopefully that little tidbit will help you understand and remember the word integrity.

Now let's go further up on Bloom's taxonomy into applying, analyzing, and evaluating. There's a story of a mother asking Gandhi to tell her son to not eat sugar. Gandhi told them to come back in a week. The family returned, and Gandhi told the boy to not eat sugar. The mother wanted to know why they had to wait a week when he could have told the boy the same thing the week before. Gandhi said that he couldn't tell the boy to stop eating sugar the week before, because Gandhi too was eating sugar. As in this Gandhi story, having integrity means that what we say, do, think, and feel are all the same, and they are integrated. As you look at the highest level of Bloom's taxonomy, when it comes to creating or having even greater application on the word integrity, ask yourself what you can do to apply integrity in your life. What can you do to live with more integrity in a particular area of your life?

Developing your character and your leadership abilities is something that every person can learn, and the learning can be transferred from one person to the next. This is divinative learning. Be divinative. The influence of lizard-brain and monkey-brain thinking in society is strong, constant, and all around us all day long. In your divinative learning process, start and end each day with divine-brain thinking. The process of learning is really about developing and utilizing your divine-brain the rest of the day.

There are many levels involved. It is like an upward spiral. One example we covered is seeing the divine in others. One level of seeing the divine in another might be the ability to forgive. Another level above that may be the ability to forgive and forget. Have you ever forgiven someone but kept a mental storage file? Do you have a mental database where you keep records of the offenses of another, and when you feel the urge, you pull up the file and remind the other person of her past offenses? Perhaps another level may not be to entirely forget, but at least not be tempted to relive and rehash past sins. Perhaps the level above forgiving and forgetting is pre-forgiving, as we have mentioned. Each of these character traits you choose to focus on will have many levels within them. The learning we are referring to here is a life-long journey of strengthening our character traits.

Let me strongly suggest another learning strategy. The best way to know how much you have learned thus far and to assess the level of your mastery in any content is to share/teach it over and over again. Each time you share/

teach you clarify things in your heart and mind. This would apply if you are trying to learn math as much as if you are trying to learn patience. It also helps to share/teach to people of different ages. When you try to share/teach what you are learning about patience, for example, it's a different experience trying to share/teach it to someone who is six, versus someone who is sixteen or someone who is sixty. Try it! When you share/teach you access different parts of your brain that will cement what you are studying. Share with a family member, members of your advisory board, trusted friends what you are learning and you will be amazed how much more you will learn, how quickly you will learn and how much longer you will retain the information. Remember the allegory of the oxen pull and how we need each other to help pull life's load. Everything you have learned in this book will more likely be applied only with the help of someone else—again probably someone from your advisory board.

When you commit to a goal like learning it's helpful to remember how to dramatically increase your chances of completing your goal. Consider these statistics from the American Society of Training and Development on the likelihood of achieving your goal with the help of an accountability advisor.

Probability of Completing a Goal When You:

Hear an idea you like	10%
Consciously decide to adopt the idea	25%
Decide when you will complete the goal	40%
Plan how you will achieve your goal	50%
Commit to someone else that they will do it	65%
Have a specific appointment with the person you committed to and give an accounting of your progress	95%

As we can see from the data, it is more likely that you will apply what you have learned if you solicit help from an accountability adviser to keep yourself on track. Getting to 95 percent likelihood of completing a goal is a matter of being thorough. As we commit to learning by allowing light-in and lead-out, we are filling our reservoirs of character strength as well as preparing for the next step of our character development—refining.

Refining

The fourth step in producing gold is refining. Refining is the process of removing the last of the impurities so that what remains is 99.9% pure gold. The gold is put in a crucible, and the intent is to subject the gold to enough heat that the gold will soften and eventually liquefy. Compounds are then added that would separate from the gold whatever impurities remain. There are uses of gold where higher levels of purity (99.99%) are required. The more pure the gold, the more intense is the refining process, the higher its value becomes, and the more specialized are its uses.

The parallel to the refining of gold as it relates to building character occurs in the crucible of the home. The third step of building character is learning; this is primarily a mental exercise—though it is an important and necessary step. The refining that occurs in the home takes our learning and gives us experience. It elevates our learning by taking it to the "real world." It doesn't get any more real than in the home. Just as the crucible is a container designed so the gold remains, until it is poured out, so is your family a contained organization. It can prepare all of us and keep us in a purer state. It readies us to be used in many ways.

At school you may be able to switch teachers, switch classes, or even switch schools, but in the home you get what you get. You don't choose your biological parents or siblings. Each person in your home comes with his or her own divine gifts and talents, as well as weaknesses. It's doubtful that any person in your home came with an instruction manual, return policy, warranties, or money-back guarantee. Being part of a family is strictly on-the-job training. This is the real world in every sense of the word.

In the real world of being a full-time worker, a person can be fired or laid-off. Not so at home. We all enter the world in a crucible called a family. Like the crucible used to refine gold, our families come in different sizes, styles, and material. What crucibles have in common is the ability to withstand a lot of heat. The structure of the family is designed for the refining of our character. There is no going around. The only way is through. We can't get fired, laid-off, or be a temp in a family. Once someone becomes a member of the family, they will always be a member of the family. Not death, divorce, disowning, time, distance, nor absenteeism can completely severe the family ties. The family links may be weak but never severed. In the crucible of the family, our characters can become pure gold. Usually when the word *crucible* is used as a metaphor, it is associated with pain. The crucible of the family, however, can and should be a wonderful thing. Though there can be tough times at home, refining takes place in the process of figuring out how to become a better family. In the heat of challenges, trials, triumphs, laughter, tears, experiences, and how we respond to them, we can realize how much we are growing and how much we are getting refined.

Being a great member of any family requires your complete emotional, physical, mental, and spiritual focus in the crucible of the home. Your leadership and character is refined in the home and it really can't be refined anywhere else in the same way. When we are refined in the crucible of the home, we are so much more prepared for any crucible that any of our other roles may present.

> To put the world right in order, we must first put the nation in order; to put the nation in order, we must first put the family in order; to put the family in order, we must first cultivate our personal life; we must first set our hearts right.
>
> —Confucius

I'm not suggesting that everything has to be perfect at home before you do anything else outside the home, because every person has to the ability to choose. Some family members may make wise choices and others not so wise, regardless of what you do. The question is whether or not you are individually doing your part to make your house a home. Just as an assayer can test gold ores for composition and value, so we can test the strength of our character by how well we are living out our values in our homes. Our homes will reveal to us what it is that we really believe and how much we have really learned. Our homes provide constant and immediate feedback regarding our character.

Remember the distance between heaven and hell and how heaven is having alignment between our hearts and minds. Remember the first three stages:

1. Identifying our strongest character traits and consistently being and doing what we already know we should be and do
2. Making the necessary sacrifice to more consistently live according to character and natural laws
3. Learning through diligent study

All of these involve learning primarily with the mind. Applying what we have learned about character development in the crucible of the home is learning with the heart. Hopefully you can appreciate how thorough this process is; our divine-brains will be tutored well. When we add to our character development the refinement that can be best taught in the crucible of the home, then not only is the divine-brain taught, but the heart is taught as well. There are certain life lessons that can only be learned within the walls of our homes. When our hearts and minds learn together at home, in the development of character, we can have a bit of heaven on earth. Hopefully you can gain a greater appreciation for what we mean by leadership and how leadership truly is a way of life. As you implement leadership as a way of life you will awaken your awesomeness within.

In the allegory of the combination lock, to this point we have explored what light-in and lead-out mean. We have understood growing in our personal and unseen lives, and now we have explored growth in our private or family lives. We'll examine growing in our public lives next. Like the three-combination lock that won't unlock, if we aren't striving for success in family life, we can't reach our full potential. It's analogous to getting two of the three numbers in the combination lock right—close but not quite there. Let's reiterate here that your home life may not, and doesn't have to be ideal. It may even seem hopeless at times. You can't control the choices of others, but you can have a great influence, even greater than you can imagine, if you are striving to be a leader in your home. If you are doing everything you can to create the culture you want in your home, but it's not quite there yet, be divinative, smile a lot, stay in divine-brain mode, and just stay the course. If you need to make changes, or if you make mistakes along the way, pre-forgive yourself, and get back on course. Allow the heat from the crucible of the home to remove any remaining impurities and refine your heart and mind.

Using Gold

Once the gold is refined, the next step depends on how the gold will be used. Let's pause here and take an inventory of what we have explored thus far. Let's look at the commitments you are considering making.

- Be divinative. Have your divine-brain be your dominant brain. Its intelligence, compared to the lizard-brain and monkey-brain, is as brilliant as the light of the noon-day sun compared to the moon and stars.
- Align what you feel in your heart with what you know your mind. (Distance between heaven and hell).
- Have a defense against the fires of your life that come from without as well as the diseases that comes from within. (Allegory of the tree—Bristlecone Pine and Redwood tree)
- Make a commitment to repeatedly go through the growing pains in the Zigzag Path to Growth, even if it doesn't feel good at the moment. It will, however, feel great later, as you get ever closer to realizing your mission.
- Commit to prayer or meditation and studying scriptures or other inspirational material as you begin and end each day in the divine-brain mode.
- See the need to work with others and lift each other's load. (Allegory of the oxen pull)
- Pre-forgive yourself so you can pre-forgive others, and keep yourself in the divine-brain mode.
- Assemble your leadership advisory board.
- Keep in mind that you have three lives: your personal life, your private or family life, and your public life or your life in the community at large. Remember, they are all important. This is the allegory of the three-combination lock.
- Approach change and improvement by allowing light-in and lead-out.
- Analyze and approach goal achievement through the Achievement Cycle. (Allegory of the four seasons)
- Identify your strongest character traits, and be consistent in being and doing what you already know you should be and do.

- Make the necessary sacrifices of yourself and of your time to develop your character.
- As the world-class musician, athlete, or scholar with a strict regimen, makes the necessary sacrifices and is also a student of her craft, commit to learning and improving.
- Apply at home what you have learned in the building of your character.
- Like painting a masterpiece one brush stroke at a time, commit to consistently make small improvements that will help you be the person and leader you want to be.
- Commit to other insights you have gained as a result of these allegories.

Wow! As you deliberately and progressively follow through on these commitments, you are prepared to make any contribution you want to make. You are pure gold. The allegory of the golden rings is about building character. It is interesting to note that when you look at the history of the word *character*, it comes from the 14th century Greek word "kharakter," which means an engraved mark. Gold is a soft metal, which makes it easier to engrave, compared to other harder metals. As we all go through the character purifying process of identifying character traits that we want to emulate in our lives, being and doing what we already know we should (prospecting), making the necessary sacrifices to focus and improve further (mining), diligently learning and unlearning to elevate our understanding (extracting), and applying our character in the crucible of the home (refining), our hearts and minds will be sufficiently softened, allowing us to then engrave upon them the character and leadership traits that we want to live by. Such softening and the engraving of both our character and confidence onto our beings, will prepare us to make the kind of contributions we want to make to society. If, on the other hand, we are hard-headed or hard-hearted, engraving anything new on our hearts and minds may prove to be a difficult task. Have you ever found it difficult to help someone change his or her character? It's because he or she was too hard-headed and hard-hearted. There's no way around but to go through a process of softening both the heart and mind.

Here's another interesting tidbit. Consider a thin strip of metal, such as tin, for example. As you bend it back and forth, eventually the strip of metal will break in two. It is also the case when gold is worked, even though it is a softer metal. With gold, however, if you reheat and liquefy it through the refining process, the gold can regain its soft and moldable state again. Similarly, whenever you find yourself getting worked and hardened by the challenges of your day-to-day activities and feel as if you might break, keep going back to this character development process, from revisiting and being grateful for your strengths and character, to spending time and effort getting refined in the crucible of your home, and you will find that you can be softened again and have the engraved mark of character imprinted deeper in your soul. Then you can continue to make your unique contributions and be the leader you can be.

Here's one more tidbit about gold. Gold is generally too soft for practical use, so other metals are generally added to it. For example, some prefer white gold over yellow gold for jewelry. White gold is made by combining nickel or silver with the gold. Red or pink gold is an alloy combining gold with copper. Likewise, having a great character is not enough. You need to combine character with knowledge and skills. Balancing great character with great knowledge and skills gives us great confidence. That's why school and training is so important. Remember the Achievement Cycle in the allegory of the four seasons. We begin with the achievements we want. We identify the character traits we need to draw from. From there we develop and align our thoughts and feelings. Getting the results and achievements we want, requires the cultivation of our minds and talents. As the world continues to change because of technology and communication, part of your leadership focus needs to be allotted to the development of your mind.

> Learning is a treasure that will follow its owner everywhere.
>
> —Chinese Proverb

Like combining other metals with gold to create a usable alloy, combining character with knowledge and skill development will allow you to be a great leader and make significant contributions.

Chapter Quiz:

Draw lines matching the five processes to make use of gold with the five processes for the development of your character.

Extracting
Make the necessary sacrifices so you can make time to focus on the development of your character

Use of Gold
Identify you strongest character traits

Prospecting
Study and learn to make your character traits even stronger.

Mining
Diligently apply your character strength at home.

Refining
Apply your character strengths in all your roles.

What are the percentages associated with the probability of completing a goal?

Hear an idea they like	_____%
Consciously decide to adopt the idea	_____%
Decide when they will do it	_____%
Plan how they will do it	_____%
Commit to someone else that they will do it	_____%
Have a specific appointment with the person they committed to and give an accounting of their progress	_____%

CHAPTER THIRTEEN

THE MIND OF A LEADER

IN the beginning of the book you were given a quick definition and overview of leadership. Here again is our definition of leadership.

> *Leadership is lifting others to the standards you are inspired to earnestly live.*

Along with a definition you were also given a visual model of our definition of leadership.

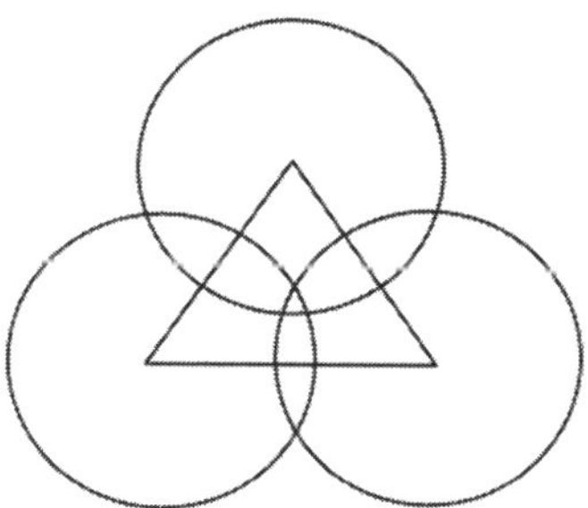

To help you understand this model more deeply we went over two sets of concepts. The first of set of concepts were:

- Three Brains
- The Ugly Duckling
- The distance between heaven and hell
- Pre-forgiveness
- The Weave of Life: To-be and To-do

The second set of concepts was specific strategies that were illustrated through allegories. The allegories were:

- Allegory #1 The allegory of the trees
- Allegory #2 The allegory of the oxen pull
- Allegory #3 The allegory of the three-combination lock
- Allegory #4 The allegory of the four seasons
- Allegory #5 The allegory of the five golden rings

There is a sixth allegory which pertains to everything we have covered and will cover. We'll go through the sixth allegory last. As we cover 1) The Mind of a Leader, 2) The Integrity of a Leader, 3) The Heart of a Leader, and 4) The Legacy of a Leader, we will draw from these two sets of concepts.

To have The Mind of a Leader as we have defined it, as a leader you need to do two things;

- Be divinative
- Choose your standards wisely

Be Divinative

Having The Mind of a Leader means you need a set of standards to live by. How will decide what your standard will be? You first need to be divinative. You will have lizard-brain and monkey-brain and divine-brain voices clamoring for your attention. From amongst all these voices use your internal voice of character to choose divine-brain voices as your dominant voice. As you consistently listen to divine-brain voices, over time these voices will be the standards you will have as a leader.

Lizard-brain and monkey-brain voices have their place and they need to be developed, but neither one can be your dominant voice. When the lizard-brain or monkey-brain are the dominant voice they only give fleeting satisfaction, and misery usually follows. For example, although it's good to win, if you think primarily in terms of winning and conquest so that you always strive to win at the expense of somebody losing, after a while no one will want to be around you anymore. Or, if you are monkey-brain dominant and are only motivated by doing whatever it takes simply to fit in, after a while your friends will know you don't stand for much. Your friends will realize that your standards are monkey-brain motivated. In other words, you don't have strong standards that are divine-brain motivated. If you are motivated only by doing what feels good at the moment, again, you don't have strong standards. The possibilities presented by your monkey-brain are tempting for the moment, but in the long run they never work.

Choose Your Standards Wisely

From among all the divine-brain voices from which you can select your standards, I would recommend you start with three; first, realize you are noble and strong like the swan in the fairy tale of *The Ugly Duckling* and have the power to make choices. I would recommend that your second standard be pre-forgiveness and the third would be to continually increase you capabilities.

Going back to the fairy tale of *The Ugly Duckling*, you are noble and strong from birth. Your greatest power is the power to choose. If the ugly duckling had not chosen to fly with the swans even when he realized he was a swan, he never would have had the experiences that made him say

I never dreamed of such happiness as this, while I was an ugly duckling.

Too many are simply content to not exercise their power to choose because it feels safer. It is safer, but you also rob yourself of the opportunity to soar and realize your leadership potential.

When you exercise your power to choose, from time to time you will make mistakes. That is why pre-forgiveness is recommended as well. Pre-forgive yourself. Know that occasionally there are setbacks. Believe in the very best, the very noble, and the very divine in you, and know you can bounce back from setbacks. Remember the allegory of the trees. Maybe you didn't come from the best of situations like the redwood tree. So what? You still have greatness in you like the bristlecone pine that lives to be around five thousand years old. The bristlecone pine lives longer than the redwood tree even though it grows in harsh conditions. Pre-forgive yourself and choose to keep moving forward.

The third standard I recommend you adopt is to continually increase your capabilities. Increasing your capability basically means lifting yourself mentally, physically, and emotionally. Regarding mental lifting, I wish someone would have told me as a teenager that school is about learning *how* to think and not just *what* to think. School teaches you *how* to think by using different subjects including math, history, technology, art, and science to tap into different parts of your brain. It's like exercising different muscles to improve overall health. School is sort of like exercising different brain muscles to improve your overall thinking skills.

When you talk to people who have their master's degrees and doctorate degrees, they'll tell you that the biggest reward they got from their degrees was learning how to think. When you talk to successful people in many industries, part of what makes them successful is learning how to think to solve problems when others don't even want to take the time to understand the problem. School is awesome once you figure what the purpose of school work is. To increase your mental capability commit to doing well in school and it will help you for the rest of your life. As you are going through tough parts of school just remember the Zigzag Path to Growth.

Figure 4: ZIGZAG PATH TO GROWTH

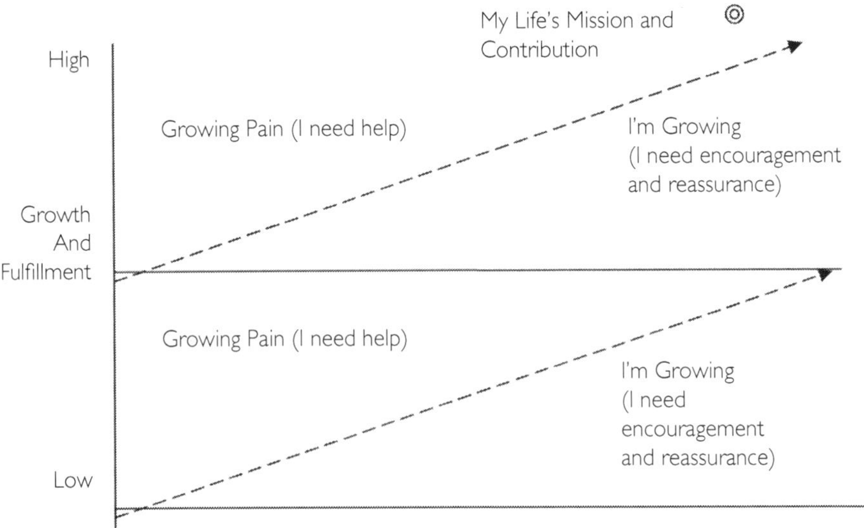

When it comes to increasing your capabilities physically and emotionally, let me give you a list of ideas to get you thinking. I'm sure you can come up with more ideas, and please do. The key is to increase your mental, physical, and emotional capabilities consistently.

Increasing Your Emotional Capabilities

Laugh	Assemble your advisory board
Visit a friend	Reach out to neighbors
Build Relationships	Take time to celebrate small successes
Smile a lot	Understand other cultures
Compliment Others	Do random acts of kindness

Increasing Your Physical Capabilities

Exercise	Relaxation	Drink enough water
Get enough sleep	Stretching	Eat a balanced diet
Dance	Walk your dog	Set fitness goals
Ride a bike	Hike	Mow the lawn

In addition to the power to choose, pre-forgiveness, and increasing your capabilities, there are many noble and divine characteristics from which to choose. You will need more than the three that was recommended. You will need a balanced set. Choose those that you appreciate in others and would want to emulate in your own life. It is one thing to choose character traits from a random list, but it's something different to choose character traits having the people to personify them. Consider what your advisory board would identify as the character traits you already possess. What characteristics come naturally and easily to you, and what aspects of your personality do you want to continue to develop?

Personality Traits:

Honest	Courageous	Charitable	Diligent
Humble	Fun	Trustworthy	Goal Oriented
Virtuous	Organized	Knowledgeable	Great Listener
Brave	Visionary	Disciplined	Energetic
Loving	Innovative	Capable	Giving
Integrity	Patient	Smart	Positive Attitude
Reverent	Creative	Action Oriented	Kind
Respectful	Pre-forgiving	Cheerful	Loyal
Hopeful	Competent	Thankful	Power to Choose

This list is not intended to be complete, but just a list to get you thinking of options. As you consider which character traits you will select ask yourself this question, "If I could choose four to six words that I would want my life to stand for, what would I choose?" If trying to choose four to six sounds a bit overwhelming at first, it's not a big deal. Start with exercising your power to choose, pre-forgiving, and increasing your capabilities. Then, add more character traits later as you feel more comfortable.

(1) The Mind of a Leader, (2) The Integrity of a Leader, (3) The Heart of a Leader, and (4) The Legacy of a Leader are all important, and they are sequential. You cannot skip steps. You cannot change the order. The Mind of a Leader and The Integrity of a Leader are about leading yourself. The Heart of a Leader and The Legacy of a Leader are about leading others. You have to lead yourself before you can lead others. When leading yourself you have to have your chosen standards first before you can have the integrity to carry out and live your standards. When leading others, those you lead need to know and feel that you care about them as people. They also need to trust you before they will allow you to lead them to the standards you are inspired to earnestly live.

Leadership, as we have defined it, begins with The Mind of a Leader. The words you choose as your standards will affect the other parts of leadership. If you don't deliberately choose yours standards *they will be chosen for you* simply by the amount of lizard-brain and monkey-brain messages you see and hear every day, constantly. You can and will probably adjust your standards as your insights change—but start now, and choose your standards wisely.

As a beginning point, think about and then write down four to six words you would choose as the standards to represent you as a person and as a leader.

____

____

____

____

____

____

Chapter Quiz:

To have The Mind of a Leader as we have defined it, a leader has to do two things:

Be __________________
Choose _____ ____________ _____________

CHAPTER FOURTEEN

THE INTEGRITY OF A LEADER

IN the last chapter you were reminded about the importance of the three brains and pre-forgiveness, and the impact they can have. It was a shorter chapter because although The Mind of a Leader is an important topic, developing The Mind of a Leader is a short process. It is simply choosing wisely the few words that would represent the standards you want to live by. The full impact and power behind the idea of The Mind of a Leader will be realized as we go through The Integrity of a Leader. In your development as a leader, take those few words that represent your personal standards and integrate them in every area of your life daily.

In this chapter on the integrity of the leader, there will be a focus on two allegories—the allegory of the four seasons and the allegory of the oxen pull. Just as The Mind of a Leader chapter focused on two actions (be divinative and choose your standards wisely) The Integrity of a Leader will also focus on two corresponding actions.

- Integrate
- Account

Before giving you specific things to do to integrate your chosen standards in your life, it will be important to do a quick review of the allegory of the Four Seasons and more specifically the Achievement Cycle.

INTEGRATE

In the Achievement Cycle, significant changes in what we are able to achieve begin with making changes or improvements in the voice we listen to.

Remember, in the Achievement Cycle the voice we listen to is the first season or the winter season. Winter is the season of new light. Winter is the season of reflection. Paying attention to the voice you will integrate into your life as a leader is a season of new light. Thinking deeply about how to integrate the voice that will dominate your thinking will require a season of reflection.

ACHIEVEMENT CYCLE

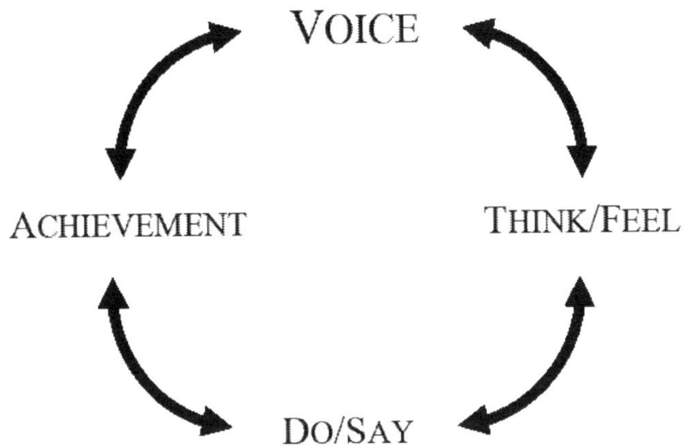

Initially, we discussed sorting through all the external voices and figuring out which ones are lizard-brain focused, monkey-brain focused and divine-brain focused. What we want to do now is to greatly influence the external voices around us instead of the other way around where the external voices are influencing us. With these action items you can turn down the lizard-brain and monkey-brain voices in your life and turn up the divine-brain voices. As you make changes regarding the voice you listen to and move clockwise in the Achievement Cycle, you will improve and increase your leadership and ultimately your achievements. These action items will not be a complete list but will give you a great start, and you will come up with even greater ideas on your own, customized for your specific situation, to integrate into your life.

Shifting to a divine-brain focus is really very easy to understand and remember. It starts with choosing what information comes in through your:

- Eyes
- Ears

It really is that simple to begin. However, don't think that because it's simple, it's not important. People who are lizard-brain and monkey-brain dominant were greatly influenced by what their eyes see on a consistent basis and what their ears listen to over and over again. So let's get started with The Integrity of a Leader and how it happens.

First of all, think about the four to six words you wrote down at the end of the last chapter that you would want to represent you as a person and as a leader.

Let's assume that you wrote as your standards you want to live by:

Fun	Loving	Power to Choose
Creative	Capable	Pre-forgiving

If, for example, you decided that these are the six words you wanted as the standards you are inspired to earnestly live, how would you integrate them in your life? Pay attention to those things that you look at and look for. Pay attention to those things you listen to and choose not to listen to. Make a list of those things you look at and listen to every day. Consider the following.

What do your eyes see?

- What books do you read?
- What pictures do you look at?
- What magazines you browse through?
- What does your room look like?
- What kinds of pictures do you have hanging in your room?
- What websites do you frequently visit?
- What computer games do you play?
- What are the apps that interest you?
- What do you pay attention to when you are walking outside?

What do your ears hear?

- What is the topic of the lyrics in the music you listen to?
- What are the subjects of your longer conversations with friends?

- What do you pay attention to when family members speak?
- What kinds of advice do you pay attention to or ignore?
- Who do you like to listen to and what kinds of things do they say?
- What kinds of movies do you watch?
- What TV shows do you watch?

As you look at the list of things your eyes see and your ears hear every day, which ones encourage you to live according to your chosen standards, and which ones do not? Go back to the six words you wrote down at the end of the last chapter and consider how they are impacted by your list of what your eyes see and your ears listen to daily. Can you identify which ones you should keep and which ones you need to get rid of?

Eyes: Notice what visually attracts your attention. What would you change and what would you keep the same? Is there anything that you would add or take away? If fun is important to you and one of your favorite fun activities is participating in a particular sport, you may have a picture of a favorite athlete in your room. You may have your trophies displayed from your sport. You may display pictures of you and your teammates in your room.

How does your bedroom visually reflect your standards as a leader? If people who don't know you came into your room, what evidence would they see that would let them know that you are a leader? Would they be able to identify the standards that are important to you? What would you put up on the walls? What would you take down?

____

____

____

Ears: Be selective and careful with what you listen to. What voices do you literally listen to? Are the music and its lyrics, conversations, teachers, heroes that you listen to saying those things that are in alignment with your self-chosen standards? Of all the external voices that come in through your ears, which would you change or add and which would you keep as is?

___

___

___

Having The Integrity of a Leader begins with information that comes in through your eyes and ears. Once voices come in, they have an impact in your heart and mind. Consider the following questions.

- What do you think about when you don't have to think about anything? Do these private thoughts deliberately come from the voice of your standards, or external lizard-brain voices, or external monkey-brain voices?
- If you chose as your standards fun, loving, power to choose, creative, capable, and pre-forgiving, do your frequent feelings (heart) reflect your standards?

Again, choose your standards, pay attention to what your eyes see, and pay attention to and be selective as to what your ears hear. This will impact how you feel in heart and what you think in your mind. The next thing you want to pay attention to are your

- Hands
- Feet
- Mouth

Whatever information you take in through your eyes and ears is processed in your heart and mind. What is processed in your heart and mind and stays in your heart and mind will manifest itself in your hands, feet, and mouth. In other words, what your heart deeply feels and your mind often considers will affect your actions (hands)—what you will do and what you will choose not to do. What you feel and think deeply in your heart and mind will impact the places where you choose to go (feet) or choose not to go, as well as the words and tone that will come out of your mouth. This cycle is true whether the actions are good or bad. A lizard-brain dominant person will take in through their eyes and eyes lizard-brain information and it will impact what they do (hands), where they go (feet), and how they speak (mouth) accordingly. A divine-brain dominant person will have a completely different set of inputs through their eyes and ears and consequently different types of results. Where a person goes (feet), what they do in those places (hands), and how they speak consistently (mouth), will determine their achievements or failures.

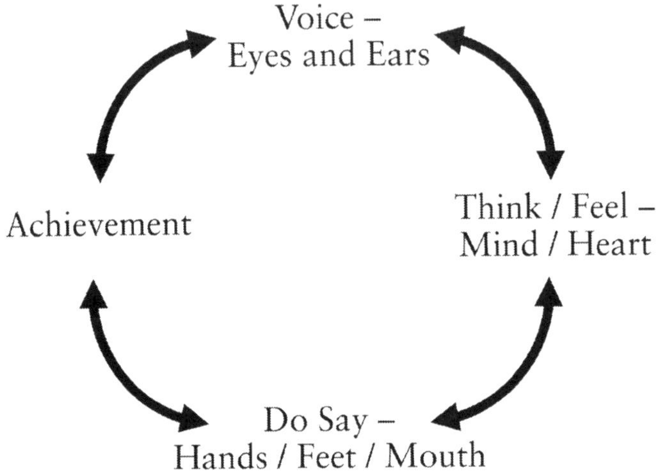

As you get results with each cycle in the Achievement Cycle, compare your achievements with your chosen standards and what you took in through your eyes and ears. If you like the results keep doing what you are doing. If not, change what you take in through your eyes and ears. With each turn you take and as you make divinative adjustments you will gain wisdom.

Having The Integrity of a Leader requires going through this Achievement Cycle consistently and deliberately. With each cycle your insights will increase. As you apply what we have covered in this chapter and live with The Integrity of a Leader, you will learn with your mind and understand in your heart your voice of character and your divine and noble nature. You will also learn what activities will prepare and inspire you to always be divinative.

Personally, some of the insights I have learned from going through the Achievement Cycle over the years I have shared with you already. These include: prayer, meditation, reading scriptures, and reading inspirational literature first thing in the morning and the last thing at night. Continually moving up the Zigzag Path to Growth—or doing things that are at least somewhat uncomfortable, such as your math problems, is another insight.

These have helped me and others to live according to our chosen standards. You will have your own profound insights that will work for you as you go through this cycle.

ACCOUNT

I mentioned earlier in this chapter that the two actions you need to take to strengthen your integrity as a leader are *integrate* and *account*. We've discussed integrate; now let's consider account. Integrating your self-chosen standards is so important because without integrating your standards they will be weak. Without The Integrity of a Leader the mind of the leader is compromised. Without The Integrity of a Leader you are not leading yourself. If you are not leading yourself you won't be effective in leading others. So much is at stake when you integrate your standards. This is why the word *integrate* is balanced with the word *account*.

In the allegory of the oxen pull we talked about the need to have an advisory board. To increase your integrity as a leader it is important that you select an advisory board member to help you. If you recall in the allegory of the golden rings we mentioned the probability of completing a goal. Having an accountability advisor gives you a 95% probability of completing your goal. Without the accountability it can be as low as 10%. You need an accountability advisor. Going through the Achievement Cycle will be slow at first and you will have questions. Get help from your accountability advisor. You will have insights and triumphs as you go through this cycle. Share and celebrate them with your accountability advisor.

Probability of Completing a Goal When You:

Hear an idea you like	10%
Consciously decide to adopt the idea	25%
Decide when you will complete the goal	40%
Plan how you will achieve your goal	50%
Commit to someone else that they will do it	65%
Have a specific appointment with the person you committed to and give an accounting of your progress	**95%**

Let me summarize what it means to have The Integrity of a Leader.

- Pay attention to what comes in through your eyes and ears.
- Follow the Achievement Cycle and pay particular attention to what words comes out of your *mouth*, where your *feet* take you, and what actions you take (*hands*).
- Get help from an accountability advisor so that you will be consistent in living according to your chosen standards.

In the last chapter you will be introduced to a powerful and simple tool that will help you integrate and account for your self-chosen standards on a weekly basis. At this point we have covered The Mind of a Leader and The Integrity of a Leader. Together this will help you to lead yourself. As you lead yourself you will be prepared to lead others. We will begin to cover that topic in the next chapter.

Chapter Quiz

The two actions to strengthen your integrity as a leader are _________ and ___________.

Strengthening your integrity requires paying attention to the information that comes in through your _______ and __________.

The information that comes in through your eyes and ears are processes in your _________ and ________.

What you truly have in your heart and think deeply in your mind will show up through your ____ (words), _____(actions), and ______(the places you go).

To increase your integrity and help hold you accountable to live according to your standards you need an _________ ___________.

CHAPTER FIFTEEN

THE HEART OF A LEADER

IN the previous two chapters, we examined the process of leading yourself. In the next two chapters we'll cover the topic of leading others. Leading others begins with having The Heart of a Leader. Having The Heart of a Leader means that what other people see and hear *from you* inspires them to trust you and gives them confidence in the standards that you earnestly live.

Remember that having The Integrity of a Leader begins with paying attention to what *your* eyes see and what *your* ears hear. As you develop the first two parts of leadership you are preparing to lead others by your example. Having The Heart of a Leader begins with what others see *you* do or don't do and begins with the words and tone *you* speak or don't speak. In previous chapters you looked to models, heroes, mentors as examples of external voices who are divine-brain dominant. As you develop as a leader you will now be somebody else's external voice. You will now be the example of someone who is divine-brain dominant. Being an external voice to another person is a great opportunity for you. There are so many lizard-brain and monkey-brain examples in the world today, that we can never have enough divine-brain examples.

Recall from The Mind of a Leader we listed two action items—be divinative and choose your standards wisely. In The Integrity of a Leader, we also had two action items—integrate and account. In this chapter regarding The Heart of a Leader our two action items are

- Love
- Lift

If you can remember and focus on these two words you will capture the spirit and intent of what it means to have The Heart of a Leader. To be more specific about what you can do to have The Heart of a Leader, consider the following.

- Listen
- Have The Integrity of a Leader
- Pre-forgive others/Focus on their potential
- Words and acts of kindness
- Keep promises

Listen

One of the greatest things we can do to lift others as leaders is to truly listen with the intent to understand them more deeply. When you look at the history and the origin of the word *listen*, you will find that it means to *hear splendor and honor*. Listen also means to *hear glory*. Imagine how our conversations would be different if we listened with the intent to hear splendor, honor, and glory. We would be less inclined to listen with the intent of fixing someone or solving her problems, because we are first trying to appreciate how wonderful she already is.

One of my favorite activities growing up was going to the beach. Swimming in the ocean, and particularly, playing in the waves was a lot of fun. Every now and then the waves would get pretty big and sometimes you would lose control. When you lost control in these ocean waves, the waves would just toss and turn you to the point that you didn't know which way was up and which way was down. You would just hold your breath until you were in shallow waters and the waves had slowed down enough that you could touch the ground, stand up, and catch your breath. The whole time you were being tossed by the waves you only thought about two things—when will this stop and when can you breathe again? You didn't think about anything else. You didn't think about family, friends, school, work, how you looked, what other people thought of you, your grades, or anything. You just wanted to know when the waves would stop throwing you around and when you could catch your next breath.

I mention this story to point out that when we don't have physical air, nothing else matters. The same is true for emotional air. When we don't have emotional air nothing else matters. The reason why listening is listed as the first thing you can do to improve your heart as a leader is because all of us need that emotional air as much as we need physical air. All of us sometimes feel like we have lost control; we don't know which way is up or which way is down. We just want to know when our loss of emotional air will stop and when we can catch our breath again.

Here's another way to realize how important listening is. As you think back to some of the conversations you hear at school, do you sometimes hear a lot of drama? The more you listen to drama the more it sounds like an unsolvable puzzle. Drama is like being tossed about in the waves of life. What if you listened not just for the words but paid attention to what the person behind the words might be going through?

> Every communication is a loving response or a cry for help.
>
> —Author Unknown

Listening gives others emotional air and is an expression of love and desire to lift another. Listening with the intent to hear honor, splendor, and glory means understanding the whole person and not just the words. Have you ever had someone see you and understand you in a better light than you were seeing yourself? What were they looking at or listening to—just your words? I don't think so. As you listen to others, listen beyond the words and beyond the drama; listen for honor, splendor, glory, and potential. You will marvel at the improvement in your relationships as you deliberately listen.

Have the Integrity of a Leader

Having The Integrity of a Leader is something we have already covered, but it's worth reminding you that the example you set as a leader matters. People are watching you (eyes) and listening to you (ears) even when you or they least expect it.

I remember conducting a seminar with a group of college-bound students. The training happened during a hot and humid summer and some were dressed immodestly. During our lunch break in one of the tables, the conversation turned to what dressing modestly meant and what dressing immodestly meant. There were about ten people around this table- young men and young women. I could also tell other teenagers from other tables were trying to listen to this conversation just like me. I was curious to know where the conversation would go.

My friend and work colleague, William Blackford IV was facilitating the conversation. He was telling the young women in particular that modesty or immodesty is a matter of where you draw attention. Modesty is when you draw attention from the neck up. The "real you," William said, is from the neck up. If you dress in such a way that you draw undue attention from the neck down, you might be dressed immodestly. This applies to the young men as well as the young women. If you only draw attention from the neck down you are not giving people the opportunity to get to know the deeper, noble, and divine you. Sometimes teenagers compete (lizard-brain) with other teenagers for attention by the way they dress. Attention or fitting in (monkey-brain) is extremely important as a teenager. Some may win the attention competition by dressing immodestly but it may not be the attention worth winning. William captured it best when he said, "How you dress will determine how you will be addressed!"

I have never heard of modesty being explained this way before and it was impressive. William was simply living according to his self-chosen standards and was trying to lift others to those same standards, but it had a profound impact on the teenagers during that seminar, on me, and now I share it with you.

Pre-Forgive Others/Focus On Their Potential

Pre-forgiveness is another topic we have already covered. You will begin to realize how impactful this idea of pre-forgiveness is for others only after you have experienced pre-forgiving yourself. In a world where so many are lizard-brain and monkey-brain dominant, people feel so much pressure to do certain things and be a certain way. When people make mistakes and the person feels under attack and not just their mistakes, it's very tough and depressing. Again, pre-forgiveness is separating the person from the mistake. There are consequences for mistakes but the person is still a person of great worth, potential, and nobility. When we pre-forgive others it is a great expression of love and a desire to lift another. As we pre-forgive others we focus on their potential or who they can yet be (future) and not just on their mistakes (past).

Words and Acts of Kindness

In the teenage world and in the adult world alike, put downs and sarcastic comments are spoken so frequently and skillfully it is almost seen as an art form. Too much of what happens in comedy shows centers on saying mean things toward or about another person. When you hear mean and degrading comments on television and then listen to laughter on the background, it sends a message that these put-downs and sarcastic comments are acceptable. If you have ever heard mean and sarcastic things said about you, however, you know it doesn't feel good and is not acceptable. Unfortunately, negative words are spoken too often and we don't get enough practice saying kind words.

To give you some practice saying kind words, let's give you some preparation. Think about one of your best friends and write his or her name down.

One of my most awesome friends is ____________________________.

Now write down ten strengths or character traits that you appreciate most about that person.

________________________ ________________________

________________________ ________________________

________________________ ________________________

________________________ ________________________

When it comes to words and acts of kindness, one of your options is to tell your friend the strengths and character traits that you appreciate about him or her. This is a wonderful opportunity to develop The Heart of a Leader. Just make sure you do this with the sole intent to let that person know that you appreciate him or her. The response will vary from person to person. Your friend may say, "thank you." Others may disagree because they don't think they are as great as you say. The reason for this type of response is because it's hard for most of us to recognize our own strengths. We assume everyone has the same strengths. We all have different strengths and different combinations of strengths. When you let others know the strengths that you appreciate about them it affirms them. You acknowledge the divine and noble in them. You will lift them up.

Keep Promises

Another recommendation is to keep promises. When you keep your promise to another person it shows two things. First it shows that *you* are a person of integrity. Remember, we said having integrity means what you say, think, feel and do are all the same. When you keep promises people will know that what you say you will do is what you will actually do. The second thing that keeping promises shows is that you value the other person enough that you will come through on your promise. Therefore, be careful when you make promises—and when you make them, keep them.

There's nothing in this chapter that is difficult to understand or that you've never heard before. A big part of being a leader is being consistent. Live with integrity toward other people, and you will develop your heart as a leader. People will trust you and know the standards that are important to you. The ideas in this chapter are by no means a complete list. The intent is to get you thinking of other actions that would fit you. What else would you add to develop your heart as a leader?

Chapter Quiz

The two actions for The Heart of a Leader are ________ and ____________.

To listen means to hear _________, _________, and __________.

Choose a family member and write down strengths and character traits that you appreciate about him or her and then let him or her know.

________________________ ________________________

________________________ ________________________

________________________ ________________________

CHAPTER SIXTEEN

THE LEGACY OF A LEADER

WE have covered leading ourselves by first having The Mind of a Leader and choosing the standards we want to live by wisely. We then lead ourselves by having The Integrity of a Leader and integrate our standards through our daily living with the help of an accountability advisor. In the previous chapter we covered The Heart of a Leader, which is the first half of being able to lead others. Only after we have The Mind of a Leader, The Integrity of a Leader, and The Heart of a Leader, are we prepared for the work and The Legacy of a Leader. The action words for The Legacy of a Leader are

- Innovate
- Unify

Innovate combined with *unify* basically means coming up with new ideas in such a way that everyone involved feels a part and the results of their work together unites them as a group. Figuring out how to lead others can be challenging because we all have different opinions. Each person interprets the world differently enough that each person has his or her own ideas of what needs to be done and how to do it. The Legacy of a Leader is not to make everyone the same but to take their differences and through their differences come up with innovative answers. The Legacy of a Leader is to innovate and unify, not once, but over and over again. The latest innovation might be great but in a world where there are constant and changing challenges, the leader needs to continue to innovate and unify. This is why the chapter is called The *L*egacy of a Leader as opposed just the leader's *current* work. Too often, instead of innovate and unify, leaders might settle for compromise and tolerate. When we say l*egacy,* we mean contribution and a lot of work. It takes effort and concentration and the effort is well worth it.

Let me give you one cheesy example. You may have seen old commercials of Reese's Peanut Butter cups. Two strangers initially argue after an accident mixes their two snacks together. One says to the other, "You have peanut butter on my chocolate." The second person then replies, "You have chocolate on my peanut butter." When they both taste the combined chocolate and peanut butter snack, they love the new discovery, and they become good friends.

In many ways this represents what happens in leadership. Two people come together; they have different points of view and strong opinions. If at least one of them is willing to pre-forgive, listen (hear honor, splendor, and glory) with The Heart of a Leader, work toward a new and better solution, they will usually come up with a better solution, and the relationship will be better for it.

Innovation always begins as a messy process. An effective leader, however, is able to work through all the mess, gains clarity, and then channels the group toward a very clear goal. How does a leader do this? As we have mentioned already, a leader must have the pre-requisites—The Mind of a Leader, The Integrity of a Leader, and The Heart of a Leader. If a leader is earnestly striving in these areas then she's prepared to tackle leading others. The components to innovate and unite are

- Have The Heart of a Leader
- Identify the real problem
- Come up with many ideas, including the crazy ones
- Work toward your best idea, then choose and implement it knowing you can and will improve on it
- Make adjustments as needed (remember you're pre-forgiven)
- Celebrate

Without The Heart of a Leader, what follows won't work as well. It is possible to come up with innovative solutions and do it in such a way that divides people. We want to innovate *and* unite.

When it comes to identifying the real problem when you have messy points of view, let me share a true story about the Jefferson Memorial in

Washington, D.C. The custodial staff of the Jefferson Memorial had a big challenge. The exterior of the Jefferson statue was deteriorating. Remember this is a national monument. This problem had to be solved. If you were the leader what would you do? What their staff did was to ask a simple question.

Why? Why was the exterior of the Jefferson memorial deteriorating? They didn't rush around coming up with answers. They wanted to first make sure they understood the problem. The more they looked into it, they found out that stronger and more abrasive cleaners were being used to clean the memorial. Again, most people would have just solved what they thought was the problem and used less abrasive cleaners. They didn't do that. Instead they asked the same question again.

Why? Why are we using stronger and more abrasive cleaners? They found out that a more abrasive cleaner was being used because there were more pigeon droppings on the Jefferson Memorial than before. They kept digging to get to the real problem and asked again.

Why? Why had there been an increase in pigeon droppings on the memorial? There were more spiders around the memorial, which then attracted more pigeons. Now what would you do? As you probably guessed, they asked the same question again.

Why? Why are there so many spiders? There were more spiders because there were more gnats than before.

Why? Why are there so many more gnats now than before? Gnats are most active at dusk. Some months prior, the lights were adjusted to turn on at dusk, and that attracted more gnats.

Now they had gotten to the real problem! The solution: turn on the lights *after* dark. Sometimes getting to the real problem means asking *why* a number of times. Just identifying the real problem is in and of itself an innovative and unifying exercise.

Let me give you another example that would be a little closer to your world. Let's assume that you are sixteen years old, and you just got your driver's license. Let's also assume that even though you have a license you don't have a car to drive. You ask your parents for a car but they don't want you to have a car. As a leader what will you do?

Remember, the first step is to have The Heart of a Leader. Listen to your parents very carefully. Recall that listening means to hear honor, splendor, and glory. Your parents have problems they want solved and you need to know what they are. Maybe you should ask them the *why* question. Why don't you think it's a good idea for me to have a car? As you dig deeper and deeper you might hear answers like

- We're concerned about your safety.
- We're concerned about the cost of having a car.
- Will you be responsible enough?
- Will you be careful and wise when you drive?

Your parents may add to this list but you get the idea. Their list only addresses half of the problem, however. You may have their concerns identified, but what about your concerns? Why do *you* want a car? Your list might include the following.

- Feeling of independence
- A sense of freedom
- Status—the cool factor
- Time with friends

Most teenagers would just try to beg their way into getting a car and they would either get the car and their parents would be worried, or the parents would say no and the teenager would feel disappointed and misunderstood. If, on the other hand, as a teenager your goal is to innovate and unify, you would work with your parents to come up with the solution that solves *both* of your concerns. Don't just come up with an answer to satisfy one list, but both! At this point you would have accomplished

- Having The Heart of a Leader
- Identifying the real problem

Now, finish the process to come up with an innovative and unifying idea.

- Come up with many ideas, including the crazy ones
- Work towards your best idea, then choose and implement it knowing you can and will improve on it

- Make adjustments as needed (remember you're pre-forgiven)
- Celebrate

I wish I could give you the magic answer to this common teenage scenario but each family is different, and each family needs to come up with an innovative and unifying solution that suits them. The process you go through to find an answer is as important as the answer itself.

Innovating while at the same time unifying is a lot of fun, but it takes practice. Start with your advisory board and practice there. I'm confident they would be willing to help you when you let them know what your intent is. It's amazing how many companies compensate and value teamwork and innovation, yet so many companies don't have the spirit of innovation and unity. The reason they don't have more innovation and unity is because people don't get much practice innovating and unifying. You will be so much more prepared when you are in your career if you can practice innovation and unity as a teenager.

One last but important aspect of innovating and unifying is to celebrate. Take time to really appreciate what you are doing well. Remember to give yourself credit for your desires as well as your efforts, even if the results are coming slower than you hoped. Celebrate even small successes. Just celebrate *everyday*! Celebrating just doesn't happen enough. Remember that having The Integrity of a Leader improves as you pay attention to the information that comes in through your eyes and ears. When celebrations occur after people innovate and unify celebration lifts the hearts and minds and encourages everyone to innovate and unify even more. The subtitle of this book encourages you to awaken your awesomeness within. As you take a leadership role in innovating and unifying, you not just awaken your own awesomeness but the awesomeness of others as well.

In review, here's a quick glance at the main action items with The Mind of a Leader, The Integrity of a Leader, The Heart of a Leader, and The Legacy of a Leader.

The Mind of a Leader

Be Divinative
Choose Your Standard

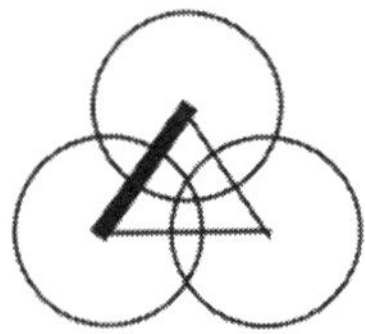

The Integrity of a Leader
Integrate
Account

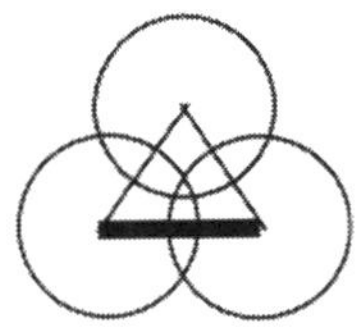

The Heart of a Leader

Love
Lift

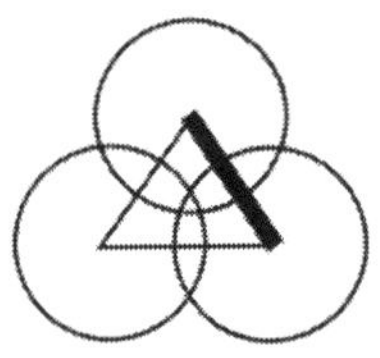

The Legacy of a Leader
Innovate
Unify

CHAPTER SEVENTEEN

LEADERSHIP SCENARIOS

ONE way to understand and gain a greater appreciation for leadership as we have defined is to see what happens when the leadership model is not followed. First let's take a look at our leadership model when it works as it is designed.

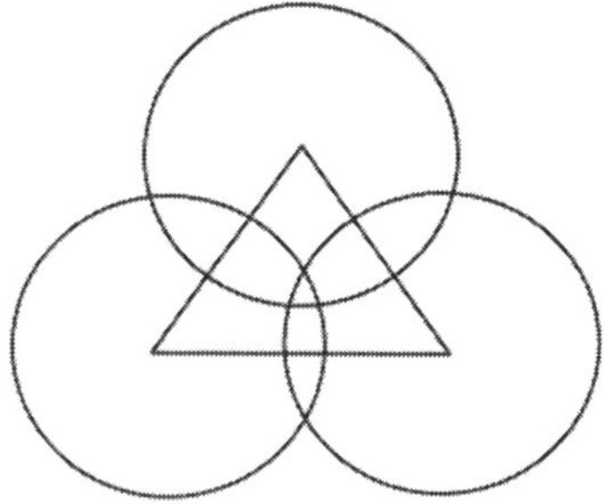

Previously, you have seen some of the models that do not work.

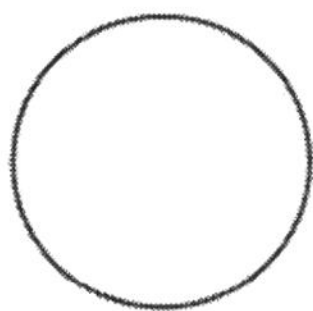

This represents someone with a lizard-brain focus. It's all about me and my survival and well-being. This doesn't work long-term. It's just one circle and nothing else.

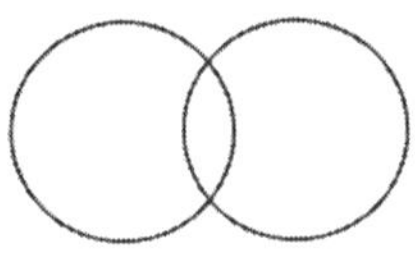

These two circles represent someone with a monkey-brain focus where relationships and feeling good is important but not connected to any effective standard. Have you known of people who lived their life this way? How well does it work?

You have seen the two previous models. The following models also represent leadership scenarios that don't work.

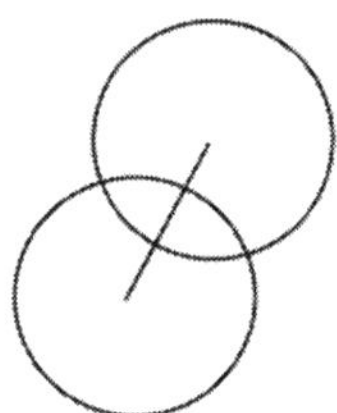

This represents individuals who understand that living according to self-chosen standards are important and have the integrity to live them, but they don't seek to lift others to those same standards.

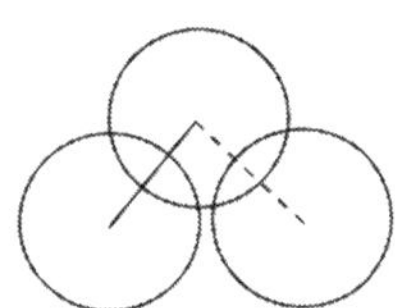

This represents individuals who have standards, have the integrity to live according to those standards, want others to live by those same standards, but don't connect with people, either because they don't want to be close or don't know how to be close; they do not have The Heart of a Leader. Without developing The Heart of a Leader it becomes more difficult to lift others to divine-brain standards. Without The Heart of a Leader you cannot realize The Legacy of a Leader.

This represents individuals with The Mind of a Leader, The Integrity of a Leader, and The Heart of a Leader, but they do not take the risk to innovate and help others become better. It's safer to not innovate and take risks, but in a fast-changing world no innovation means limited progress and unrealized potential for self and others. If you don't take the risk to innovative and unify you cannot have The Legacy of a Leader.

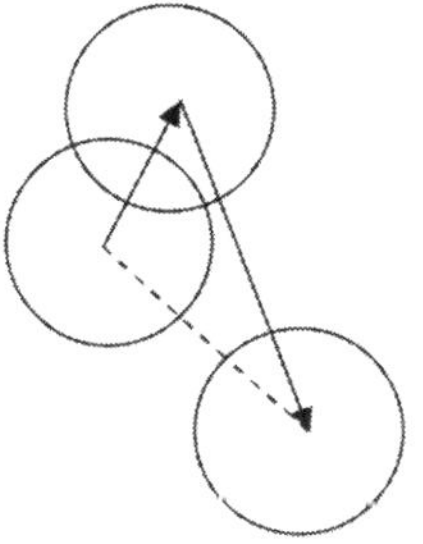

This represents ***self*** going in the direction of their chosen standards and ***others*** going away from those same standards. Notice that as the distance between ***others*** and the ***standards*** gets further apart, the distance between ***self*** and ***others*** also gets further apart. This explains why sometimes good friends who were close before drift apart. Their standards change.

You can imagine other scenarios where the mind, integrity, heart, and legacy of a leader don't follow the leadership model, and the full potential of leadership is not realized. All of these unfortunate scenarios happen sometimes, but as you develop your leadership abilities and become aware of the goal of leadership and the importance of each component of this leadership model, you will know what actions you need to take to have The Mind of a Leader, The Integrity of a Leader, The Heart of a Leader, and realize The Legacy of a Leader.

Let me give you one more scenario that will help you appreciate family members and friends for their leadership.

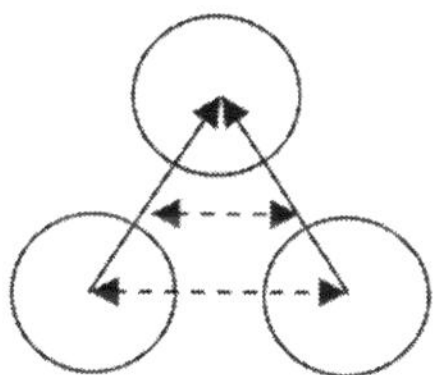

In this picture the circles are smaller because you need to pay particular attention to the lines. This picture represents you and the other person moving towards the same standards. Notice that as you and other person move closer to the standards, you are also getting closer to each other.

Isn't that cool! Having family members and friends who are willing and inspired to earnestly live by the same standards as you do is something that doesn't happen every day. So as you find those situations, be grateful for them. Love them. Keep them close. You will continually lift each other towards your standards. As you choose and seek out friends as well as a spouse someday, seek for people who have the same standards as you do and who already earnestly strive to live according to those standards with integrity.

CHAPTER EIGHTEEN

ALLEGORY #6: ACHIEVING FLIGHT

TOO often great information, even inspirational information, fades in our minds over time, but creating a process to go along with it enables our learning and transformation to endure. Our last allegory is about implementation and application.

Every time I fly, I love getting the window seat on the plane and looking out as the plane takes off. It's especially exciting when you're on the largest planes. You can feel the power of the engines as the plane accelerates down the runway. Soon after the plane is off the ground, the plane retracts the landing gear, and then without the drag of the landing gear, the flight is smoother and becomes quieter. All the while, the plane continues to lift and rise above the trees, buildings, hills, and even the highest mountains. As the plane steadily climbs, your vision expands. The morning and afternoon flights when it is cloudy and even rainy is especially dramatic. The plane climbs through the rain and clouds and then suddenly breaks through the mist of gray into the glorious sunshine. The plane continues to climb through occasional turbulence, then finally there is a smooth flight, with the feeling of perfect stillness, and you look out the plane window with unlimited visibility.

It is amazing how the take-off on a commercial flight parallels our own lives. We want our lives to take flight, and we want to position ourselves much as the plane positions itself on one end of the runway with a flight plan established. It takes a tremendous effort just to get a plane moving and gaining speed in preparation for flight. So it is with us. Resolve, effort, and persistence are required, along with our personal flight plan or mission.

Daily uplifting habits are needed for us to gain momentum and lift. Just as following the laws of flight will determine whether or not the plane will lift above clouds, darkness, and storms, and arrive at its destination, so can you and I realize our awesomeness within regardless of the storms we have to weather, if we understand and follow the laws that lift men's souls.

Throughout this book I've mentioned showing you a simple and powerful tool to take everything you have learned so far, and implement that information to help you make leadership a way of life and awaken your awesomeness within. To do so, implement the following weekly process:

- Review your life's flight plan or mission statement.
- Review you Leadership Focus pages and fill out your Weekly Attitude Indicator.
- Live in the present.
- Account to your accountability advisor.

Flight Plan or Mission Statement

Just as a plane doesn't leave the airport until the pilot has a destination and flight plan, we also need our personal flight plan for our lives. This can also be called our personal mission statement. There are many ways to do a mission statement. The correct and great mission statement is the one in which you can answer *yes* to this question:

Does it inspire me?

I've seen personal mission statements as long as twelve pages and as short as two words. I've seen mission statements in which there were no words, because they had captured their mission statements through art, a collage of pictures, music, or objects. A personal mission statement is very personal. Make it however you would like, so long as it is inspiring to you. A personal mission statement is something you revisit weekly and change as your life's experience and insights change.

For your first draft of your mission statement, however, consider the following approach. Your first draft will have four parts. They are:

- The character traits or standards you want to live by
- Your future goals and capabilities you'll need to get there
- Your vision of what you want to contribute to your family
- The contribution you want to make in your other roles as a friend, a student, in your future career, and any other roles or leadership focus you may have

That's it! Keep it that simple. Again, you'll probably change it over time, and that's okay, but this four-part first draft of your mission statement will give you a great start. Your mission statement will inspire you and it will be exciting to travel towards it. So let's get started on your first draft of your personal mission statement!

Get a folder to use in creating your leadership planner as described next. You will capture in these pages answers to some pretty important questions. You have answered some of these questions already. We just want to transfer them to one tool. On the first page you will simply answer a few questions.

- What are the character traits or standards that I want to live by and who is the best example of these particular character traits?
- What are my personal goals as a teenager, and what mental, physical, and emotional capabilities that will I need to help me get there?
- What are my personal goals when I am no longer a teenager, and what mental, physical, and emotional capabilities will I need to help me get there?
- Every member of every family contributes to the overall feeling within the family. What feeling do I want in my home and family, and how can I contribute to that feeling?
- What contribution do I want to make in the world so that the world will be better because I am in it?

Once you answer these questions ... Congratulations! By simply answering those questions you have the most important aspects of your mission statement. You have finished your first draft. Your final draft won't be finished for decades, because as your insights change your mission will adjust. However, also come up with your second draft of your mission statement. If you want the second draft of your mission statement written in words, then reread your answers you just wrote down, and while they are fresh in your mind, go to a quiet place where you can reflect and write down why those answers are important to you. You can also choose to express your mission in a different way. Again you can create a collage, draw a picture, create a painting, write a piece of music, or choose an object that would represent your mission.

You'll have one page for your first draft in your leadership folder. You'll have your second page for your second draft. On another page, write down who you would include as members of your leadership advisory board. Here's what these first three pages may look like.

MY PERSONAL FLIGHT PLAN OR MISSION STATEMENT

What are the character traits or standards that I want to live by and who is the best example of these particular character traits?

Character Trait or Standard	*Best Example: Name*
Uses power to choose	______________
Pre-forgiving	______________
Increase Capabilities	______________

What are my personal goals as a teenager and what mental, physical, and emotional capabilities will I need?

Personal Goals	*Mental, Physical, Emotional Capabilities*
______________	______________
______________	______________

What are my personal goals when I am no longer a teenager, and what mental, physical, and emotional capabilities will I need?

Personal Goals	*Mental, Physical, Emotional Capabilities*
______________	______________
______________	______________

Every member of every family contributes to the overall feeling within the family. As a leader in my home, what feeling do I want in my home and family, and how can I contribute to that feeling?

____

____

What contribution do I want to make in the world so that the world will be better because I am in it?

____

____

SECOND DRAFT OF MY PERSONAL MISSION STATEMENT

Starting with the answers I wrote down on my first draft of my mission statement, what is important to me and why?

MY LEADERSHIP ADVISORY BOARD

I have chosen to following people to be part of my leadership advisory board because they are people who

Will help me live my standards
Act in good faith
Will help me grow and develop
Will hold me accountable
Are supportive
Help me tap into my potential
Care about me
Have my best interest
Listen
Give great input and advice
Validate and affirm
Are divine-brain focused

Board Member	Reason for Selection and How He or She Can Help Me
______________________	______________________
	______________________
______________________	______________________
	______________________
______________________	______________________
	______________________
______________________	______________________
	______________________
______________________	______________________
	______________________
______________________	______________________
	______________________
______________________	______________________
	______________________

Fill Out Your Weekly Attitude Indicator

From the simplest to the most sophisticated airplanes, there are certain gauges in the instrument panel that exist in all of them. The gauge in an instrumentation panel of a plane that lets the pilot know the orientation of the plane relative to the earth is called a gyro horizon or artificial horizon. Interestingly, it is also called an attitude indicator. The attitude indicator lets a pilot know whether the plane has the nose pointed down and the plane is moving downward toward the earth below, or whether the nose is pointed up and the plane is rising. Similarly, we lift and move upward and forward toward our mission, or we can end up someplace else. Through this allegory you'll not only get a sense of where your attitude is currently heading, but also what may be causing your attitude to be great or less than ideal.

The attitude indicator will also tell a pilot when the plane is rolling or tilted to the left or right as the plane turns. If the plane continues to turn in one direction, the plane will be traveling in circles. Some commercial flights will do this on purpose while waiting to get clearance from the air traffic controller to land. This is called a holding pattern.

Have you ever felt that your life has been in a holding pattern even when you don't want to be in a holding pattern? We may have this holding-pattern feeling from time to time, where get the sense that our lives are not really moving forward, but we are using time and energy going in circles. To prevent this holding pattern feeling from happening, you need to lift your life in four areas of leadership focus:

- Lift and strengthen your character.
- Lift and increase your capabilities.
- Lift and love your family.
- Lift and work to help others.

To make sure we capture ideas on how to lift ourselves in these four leadership foci, we will have a page for each one. If you notice, strengthening your character or standards as well as increasing your capabilities will help you lead yourself and improve your *mind* as a leader and your *integrity* as a leader. Lifting your family as well as contributing in your other roles and responsibilities will help you lead others and improve your *heart* as a leader and your *legacy* as a leader. My goal is to help you remember and implement everything you have learned in this book by using a leadership tool. First, add these four *leadership focus* pages in your folder.

LEADERSHIP FOCUS: STRENGTHEN MY CHARACTER

As a leader 24/7 I will strengthen my character by developing The Mind of a Leader and The Integrity of a Leader by doing the following:

- Be divinative
- Begin and end my day with prayer or meditation and read scriptures or inspirational literature
- Pre-forgive myself along the way
- Commit to the Zigzag Path to Growth—growing pains are normal
- Assemble and get advice from my leadership advisory board
- Review the Achievement Cycle and make the appropriate adjustments
- Reduce or eliminate lizard-brain and monkey-brain activities

What else do I want to have happen that is not now happening in strengthening my character and self-chosen standards, and what should I continue doing, stop doing, and start doing to make it so?

____

____

____

____

____

____

____

____

____

____

____

____

LEADERSHIP FOCUS:
INCREASE MY LEADERSHIP CAPABILITIES

Mental Capabilities

Remember, school is about learning ***how*** to think!

Do well in school
Do school work before play
Celebrate successes in school
Zigzag Path to Growth
Ask more questions
Assemble advisory board for school

Physical Capabilities

Exercise
Get enough sleep
Dance
Ride a bike
Relaxation
Stretching
Walk your dog
Hike
Drink enough water
Eat a balanced diet
Set fitness goals
Mow the lawn

Emotional Capabilities

Build relationships
Laugh
Smile a lot
Random acts of kindness
Visit a friend
Take time to celebrate small successes
Understand other cultures
Compliment others

Additional Ideas:

____

____

____

____

____

____

____

____

____

LEADERSHIP FOCUS: BE A LEADER AT HOME LIFT MY FAMILY

- Listen with the intent to hear the splendor, honor, and glory of each member of my family.
- Be an example and have The Integrity of a Leader.
- Pre-forgive my family.
- Communicate using affirming and loving words.
- Display random acts of kindness.
- Keep promises.
- Look for opportunities to innovate and unify at home.

What else do I want to have happen that is not now happening in my family, and what should I continue doing, stop doing, and start doing to make it so?

OTHER LEADERSHIP FOCUS: LEADER AT ____________

LOVE/LIFT and INNOVATE/UNIFY IN OTHER ROLES

I will have The Heart of a Leader when I work with others.
I will remember to ***innovate*** and ***unify***.

- Identify the real problem.
- Come up with many ideas, including the crazy ones.
- Work towards the best idea, then choose and implement it, knowing you will improve on it.
- Make adjustments as needed (remember, you're pre-forgiven). Celebrate!

When I work with other people outside my home, where are my greatest opportunities to improve my heart as a leader (love and lift) and the legacy as a leader (innovate and unify)?

____

____

____

____

____

____

____

____

____

____

____

____

In implementing leadership as a way of life, follow this weekly leadership process.

- Review your life's flight plan or mission statement.
- Review your *Leadership Focus* pages and fill out your Weekly Attitude Indicator.
- Live in the present.
- Account to your accountability advisor.

So far, you have two pages for your life's plan or mission statement. You have an additional page for your leadership advisory board, and you have another four pages for each *leadership focus.* These pages capture much of the vital information in this book and will help you remember and implement them. In these *leadership focus* pages you are given additional space to brainstorm ideas and capture your flashes of brilliance that you'll want to implement when you are ready.

If you add more roles or leadership focus, include additional leadership focus pages. The ideas you brainstorm may not be something you do right away, but at least you have written it down so you won't lose the idea. Just as a plane has an attitude indicator to gauge whether it's moving up, down, or turning, you will have what is called a Weekly Attitude Indicator to do the same thing for your life. Before you fill out your weekly attitude indicator let me mention why it's a weekly and not a daily or monthly attitude indicator.

For most people a week means a seven-day period, but historically a week has ranged anywhere from a three-day to a ten-day time period in different parts of the world. The Aztecs and Maya even had a thirteen-day week. The length of the week is not as important as what the week represents. The week represents the shortest cycle of living. For our purposes we'll define the week as a seven-day period. In this seven-day cycle of living, your activities during the weekend tend to be different from your activities in the weekday. Even within your weekdays, your activities on Mondays are different from your activities on Thursdays, and so on. Think of living the life of a leader in increments of a week. Let me show you the weekly attitude indicator you will use.

WEEKLY ATTITUDE INDICATOR

Climbing left bank

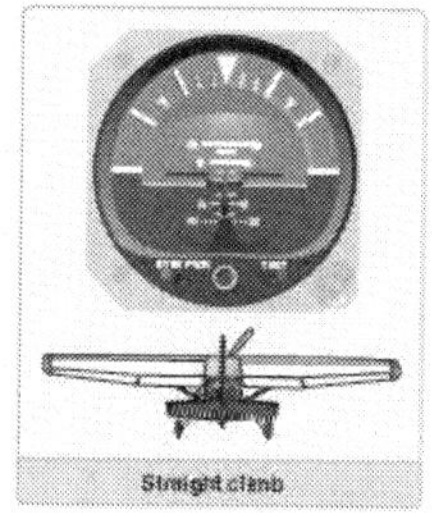
Straight climb

Climbing right bank

LEADERSHIP FOCUS AND GOALS FOR THIS WEEK

Week of: ______________ Accountability Adviser: ______________

Leadership Focus—Strengthen Character

____

____

Leadership Focus—Increase Capabilities

____

____

Leadership Focus—Lift My Family

____

____

Leadership Focus—Improve Contribution

____

____

Other Leadership Focus

____

____

Weekly Planning Process

Sometime between Friday afternoon and Sunday evening block out fifteen to twenty minutes to plan your coming week. In your planning time, first think in terms of your mission or your life's flight plan. Reconnect. Be inspired and renewed by your mission and what you want to be and do in your life. After reviewing your mission statement, review your leadership focus pages. For the coming week you may consider goals from the list you have written on your *leadership focus* pages, or by simply reviewing your list, you will probably come up with other thoughts and ideas.

Write your goals on your weekly attitude indicator. Only put one goal down for each leadership focus. Making the list longer doesn't necessarily make things better. Sometimes more is just more but not better. Ask yourself, what is the *one* best thing you can do to lift each leadership focus?

After you fill out your weekly attitude indicator, think for a moment about what your week would be like if you were able to accomplish everything on your weekly attitude indicator. If the goals you have written down are goals that you feel will truly lift your character, capabilities, your family, and will help you improve the contributions you are making in the leadership focus of your life, it will give you a sense of moving towards your mission. In those cases when you only accomplish some of the goals you have written down on your weekly attitude indicator, you should still feel pretty good, because you are making deliberate strides toward your mission. If you find that in certain weeks you are not able to finish everything you have set out to do in your weekly attitude indicator, pre-forgive yourself and try it again the following week.

After you fill out your weekly attitude indicator and you are going about life as a teenager, *live in the present.* I have a mentor who is great at telling stories about what happened in the past. He remembers everything in great detail, and as you listen to him you can almost imagine being in the story. His stories are so colorful that you might think he must be making up some of it. I thought that way until he told a story in which I had been involved. As he was telling the story he would recall things in great detail that I had forgotten. He was amazing. Asking him how he could remember so much. He said, I don't know exactly how I remember so much, but I know why *you* don't.

Startled, I asked him what he meant by that. Then he told me something that is hard to ever forget. He said, Charles, you spend so much time in the future or so much time in the past that you never live in the present. You don't have the memories I do because mentally you weren't there. You were somewhere in the future or somewhere in the past. Too often teenagers are worried about the past and the future. If you learn from the past, make leadership a way of life and awaken your awesomeness within; the future is bright. You can live in the present and treasure being a teenager.

The last step of your weekly planning process is to let your accountability adviser know how your last week went and what your goals are for the coming week. This need not be a long process. Remember that the probability of completing your goals increases to 95 percent when you have a specific appointment with your accountability adviser and give an accounting of your progress. Choose an accountability adviser whom you trust and whom is willing to help you reach your goals of becoming the person and leader you want to be. The person will probably be someone from your advisory board. Even if you just spend five minutes once a week, it will be some of the most important minutes in your week, because you are ensuring that leadership is a way of life for you. Again, here's a quick summary of your weekly process.

- Review your life's flight plan or mission statement.
- Review your Leadership Focus pages and fill out your Weekly Attitude Indicator.
- Live in the present.
- Account to your accountability advisor.

Daily Planning

After you have filled out your weekly attitude indicator, transfer your goals to your calendar. Some of your goals can be easily transferred, while other goals can't be scheduled. For example, if one of your goals is to be more patient, this is not a goal you will narrow down to a day and time, but it's something you will work on throughout the week. Schedule the goals in your weekly attitude indicator first, and then plan the remainder of the week.

I have found that daily planning will vary with each teenager's style, attention to detail, personality, extracurricular activities, and number of roles outside of home and school. The essence of daily planning is making sure you have written down all of your assignments, tests, and projects due, so you don't forget. You will also jot down your to-do list, which is not time-specific like your appointments are. After you have created your to-do list, put an "M" next to those items on your to-do list that you *must* do, an "S" next to those you *should* do and a "C" next to those you *could* do. Prioritize and number all of the items you must do, so you'll have M1, M2, M3, and so forth. Do the same thing with the should-do list and your could-do list.

Do the must-do items first, followed by the should-do list, and lastly the could-do list if you have time. Check each item off as you do it, because it feels good to check things off a list.

If you have a different process for daily planning that you like, do that. You will more than likely gravitate toward a system that feels comfortable to you for daily planning. There is more than one right way to do daily planning. Regardless of the system you use for daily planning, what is infinitely more important is meeting the goals you put in your weekly attitude indicator. Congratulate yourself for getting the big stuff done—the vital and impactful few items that lead you to your mission—and don't sweat the never-ending smaller stuff.

The leadership/time management tool we have explored in this chapter is like using a GPS. With a GPS, as you scroll out you will get a bigger perspective but less detail. As you scroll in you'll have less perspective but more detail. When you see your life through the lens of your mission statement, you'll have great perspective but not much detail. When you look at life through the lens of daily planning, you have great detail but not much perspective. Looking at your life through the lens of your weekly attitude indicator gives you the opportunity to see your life with a balanced perspective as you consider your areas of leadership focus. Between your mission statement, your weekly attitude indicator, and daily planning, which one should you use? *All three*! You want to see your life scrolling in and out through all three of these perspectives.

Wow! You made it! You have the definition of leadership. You have a picture that goes with your definition. You know the sequence of leadership beginning with The Mind of a Leader, followed by The Integrity of a Leader, The Heart of a Leader, and finally The Legacy of a Leader. You have the actions items you need to take to improve on each of these parts of leadership. You have a simple tool to take everything you have learned and implement them.

Let me close where we began. I believe will all my heart and mind that being a teenager can and *will* be the best time of your life the more you understand leadership. I am excited for your journey as you realize your awesomeness and become the leader you can and are meant to be.

I wish you all the best.

Final Exam:

Are you ready to lead?

Made in the USA
Lexington, KY
02 May 2014